Islāmic vs Postmodern Paradigm of Sexuality

(Rethinking the Rainbow)

Islamic Vs Post-Modern Paradigm of Sexuality, by Dr. Asif Hirani
ISBN: 978-1-7333114-2-7

Published by Islamic Learning Foundation
166-26 86th Ave
Jamaica, NY 114432
(315) 534 - 0790

1st Printing – May 1, 2023

Foreword

Mobeen Vaid (Muslim Public intellectual)

The Prophet (ﷺ) reportedly likened the souls of man to "conscripted soldiers," converging upon what they recognize and diverging over that which they reject. In this report, much has been written. Some, including Ibn Hajar, have speculated that those with similar temperaments and dispositions incline to one another, while others have written about the affinities of righteousness and maleficence. Whatever the case, it is clear that some people simply "sync" with one another early on. That was certainly my experience with our courageous and incisive author, Dr. Asif Hirani.

A few years ago, Dr. Hirani reached out to me interested in exploring more deeply questions undergirding public discourses surrounding gender and sexuality. Not knowing him, I agreed to speak, but did not commit to much. My time, I said, was limited, and though I was open to speaking, I could not set aside much for a sustained engagement. Soon, however, Dr. Hirani's unassuming demeanor gave way to what would become a lasting relationship, with his erudition, scholarly appetite, and deep desire for the collective welfare of the *ummah* becoming obvious, to which I could not help but gravitate towards.

In the intervening years, Dr. Hirani and I have had numerous exchanges diving deeply into the topics of sexuality and gender, and, additionally, the nature of modernity itself. What is it exactly about our world that has made these two categories of human life so central? Why is it that the conflicts surrounding them only seem to intensify and never abate? And how, as Muslims, can we navigate these topics faithfully, respond to questions persuasively, and explain why, exactly, our own commitments as Muslims seem to so often differ from the current fashions being championed in the public square?

The current work revolves around precisely these questions, synthesizing key arguments and studies, teachings and material from the redoubtable Dr. Sharif El-Tobgui, and deftly drawing upon resources from other faith traditions, particularly Christian ones, while carefully discerning between those matters that accord with Muslim belief and those that do not. This synthesis is exposited as a matter of *paradigmatic* difference: we are not merely discussing discrete differences in how we view sex or gender, but, in fact, seeking to understand what animates those controversies and differences as well as the fundamental assumptions that make modernity, modernity.

Perhaps best of all, readers will find Dr. Hirani's work eminently accessible, a resource that can easily be made use of in Islamic schools, circles of religious study, and book clubs.

We ask Allah to make this book a work of benefit for the readers, a contribution to the *ummah* that weighs heavily on the scales of good for the author, and that He unites us all upon what pleases Him, 'azza wa jal. *Ameen.*

Foreword

Sh. Abdur Rahman bin Abdil Azeez

The topic of sexuality is one that has recently been the subject of much discussion and debate, both within Islamic and postmodern contexts. As human beings, we all have a natural inclination towards intimacy and desire, but the way we approach and understand these concepts can vary greatly depending on our cultural and religious background. Not to mention that this has always been a very sensitive issue in the Muslim Community and not too many wanted to discuss it.

In his book Islāmic vs Postmodern Paradigm of Sexuality (Rethinking the Rainbow), the author Dr. Hirani courageously presents a comparative analysis of the Islamic and postmodern paradigms of sexuality. By exploring the two different worldviews, the book offers valuable insights into the way in which sexuality is understood and practiced in each context.

By examining these two worldviews, Dr. Hirani sheds light on the differences between them. The book provides a detailed analysis of the various aspects of sexuality, including its physical, emotional, and spiritual dimensions, and explores how these are understood and practiced within each paradigm.

The author's deep understanding of Islamic teachings and postmodern thought makes this book an invaluable resource for anyone seeking to understand the two paradigms of sexuality. The book is not only informative, but it is also thought-provoking, challenging readers to consider their own perspectives on sexuality and how they relate to their cultural and religious beliefs

Overall, this book is a timely and important contribution to the discourse on sexuality, providing valuable insights into two different worldviews and encouraging readers to think critically about their own beliefs and practices.

I highly recommend it to anyone interested in understanding the Islamic and postmodern paradigms of sexuality. It is so worthwhile to read.

The Preface: Rethinking the Rainbow – Islāmic vs Postmodern Paradigm of Sexuality

Godless World Covered by a Rainbow Cloud

A century ago, women in the United States were denied the right to vote, yet today we are grappling with the question: what is a woman? Societies' confusion between these two extremes is a consequence of removing God and His divine message from the social sciences; as result, society becomes like a pendulum swinging from one extreme to the other.

Moving from the extremes of masculinity/femininity towards the concept of gender fluidity removes the fundamental ability to identify and define the specific genders. This confusion has arisen now that God (The Higher Authority) and the Hereafter (a sense of accountability) have been removed from the social sciences. This results in the abandonment and removal of divine guidance. Which, in turn leads to a vacuum of 'who' objectively decides what the rights of men and women are.

Back in the day, homosexuality carried a negative social stigma in the West. It was considered morally wrong, but now, homosexuality is not only considered to be legitimate, but has become the defining feature of one's identity. Homosexuality is not just mainstream but is celebrated to the point that we are often told that being critical of the LGBTQI+ movement is being "on the wrong side of history". How did things get this way? It is surreal at times to reflect on the pace of change when it comes to the progression of the LGBTQI+ movement.

What a parent considers to be a loving response to a child struggling with same-sex attraction, or gender identity disorder, or gender dysphoria, might be regarded by the child and surrounding adults as hateful and bigoted.

Welcome to our new postmodern Godless society. As Carl Truman argues: in just one generation, popular culture has gone from questioning whether a man and a woman could be "just friends", to outright declaring the civil right of a man to become a woman. Nowadays, if one upholds that the institution of marriage can only be between a man and a woman, they are considered to be a dangerous and fringe lunatic.[1]

This brings to mind a verse from the Qur`ān, Sūrah Noor, āyah 40:

"And he to whom Allāh has not granted light - for him there is no light."[2]

One of the most poignant aspects of modern public life is the central role that sex plays. This may be jarring for our parents, and especially our grandparents, but the fact that the most private and intimate act between two people has become so important to public life is surely a strange and remarkable development. Indeed, from legislation on matters such as gay marriage & trans rights, to the apparent need of the public to know about the sexual orientation of sports athletes, actors, and celebrities, the role of sex in our culture is pervasive and unprecedented.

Why has this become the case? As we will go over in the next few chapters, in the last century, sexual feelings/desires have emerged as the primary factors in determining our identities. To put it in other words,

---

[1] Strange New World, Carl Trueman, 19-20
[2] Surah An-Noor, Verse 40

traditionally, sex was something I 'did', but now sex is something that defines who I 'am'.

Hence, we now have an ever-expanding list of letters to add to the LGBTQI+ alliance, who are defining their identity based on their sexual feelings, which is historically unprecedented.

Why did I choose to write a book on this topic?

To be quite honest, there is not enough written material available on this topic from the Islāmic scholarly perspective, except for a few articles. Thus, my aim was to provide a basic guide for Muslim and non-Muslim readers alike, to critically examine postmodern issues of sexuality from the lens of the Islāmic paradigm. This will serve to not only help the reader understand the Islāmic paradigm on sex, sexuality, and identity, but to help appreciate its beauty in contrast to the postmodern society surrounding us, by looking at loopholes in the postmodern paradigm of sex, sexuality, and identity.

There are few useful resources on this topic from conservative Biblical scholars. But a few key elements were missing in their efforts, which I would like to highlight briefly. Some of the basic differences between the Islāmic worldview and right-leaning conservative scholars or activists are:

A) Philosophical worldview vs Prophetic or Divine worldview:

Some of these conservative and Biblical scholars used Western philosophy to deconstruct arguments of sexuality, and honestly speaking, some of them are very well-thought-out. But the problem with the philosophical worldview is that Western philosophy is very good at belaboring points of contention, but often falls short in providing practical solutions, and that was what was missing from their arguments. We as Muslims must keep revelation as the supreme intellectual authority in our teachings and worldview. Yes, we should use sound reason and are permitted to use technical philosophical language to elucidate our problems, but we must then use revelation to provide tactful solutions.[3]

B) Instead of reason without revelation, it should be reason *and* revelation:

The impact of the modern world has left some conservative Christian scholars feeling uneasy about incorporating the words "God", "accountability in the hereafter", and "going back or surrendering to God's divine message", into their responses to issues of sexuality. Instead, they often rely solely on reason, logic, and science, without utilizing divine arguments or revelation. As Muslims, we believe in using both reason and revelation, but not at the expense of one over the other. If both are based on definite evidence and certain in implication and transmission, a combination of reason and revelation can provide the highest level of clarity and certainty. Furthermore, we believe that pure reason and a plain-sense reading of authentic revelation, which is certain in terms of implication and transmission, can never contradict each other.[4]

Therefore, while using science might be a great way to prove your argument, it becomes a problem if that's the only basis

---

[3] Ibn Taymiyyah, Majmoo' Al-Fatawa, Maktaba Al-Safa, Egypt, 2006, page 3:306

[4] Carl Sherif El-Tobgui, Reason, "Revelation & the Reconstitution of Rationality: Taqī al-Dīn Ibn Taymiyya"s (d. 728/1328) Dar' Ta'ārud al-'Aql wa-l-Naql or 'The refutation of the contradiction of reason and revelation', page 6

of your argument, especially in the discussion of morality because:

1) The epistemology of science doesn't deal with morality or metaphysics.
2) Science is not always as fair and objective as we might think it is, for it to be used as a proverbial yardstick.
3) Scientific research is varying and evolving all the time based on new technologies and discoveries, which should not be the case with morality.
4) Scientific research, which seems unbiased, can be tainted due to the personal agendas, motives, biases, and prejudices of scientists, or from involvement of foreign entities.

Relying solely on scientific arguments to explain morality and address contemporary issues, such as sexuality, without incorporating divine standards will ultimately fall short. This approach can lead to circular arguments, leaving us lost in a dark desert without direction or guidance. Additionally, since science is constantly evolving, a criticism made today may be resolved tomorrow. What happens then? Will we abandon our morality and adopt the constantly changing views of science in regards to morality? Rather, we must "submit and surrender" to the morality given to us by a higher power; one that possesses more knowledge and wisdom than us. We must then inculcate and apply these laws as rationally and reasonably as possible.

C) Responding to one extreme from the other:

In today's climate, extreme responses to extreme ignorance are commonplace. The far-right often responds to feminism with masculinism, and to liberalism with conservatism, causing an increase in polarization. And vice versa, because liberalism doesn't give regard to scripture, they responded to conservatism with liberalism, and to theocracy with religious abolishment. This phenomenon is further perpetuated by poorly executed polemics from social media influencers. The lack of synthesis or balance in these arguments, stemming from a deficiency in divine guidance, serves only to fuel the fire. Instead, we must return to the creator of male and female, the creator of liberals and conservatives, and approach every issue, including issues of sexuality, through the lens of divine guidance and wisdom. Islām prides itself on being a moderate or centrist religion, therefore we must strive to find a balance between extremes using reason and divine guidance to address contemporary issues.

This extreme climate is what drove me to write this book. I wanted to use arguments not just from reason, but also divine guidance. Human desire requires divine guidance, so we must dissect this issue using a proper balance of reason and revelation, giving divine guidance supreme authority.

I would say the best response so far to this issue from the Biblical scholarly perspective is by Dr. Carl Trueman.[5] I really like his approach, and I will try to use some of his work 'but' in a Sharī'ah-complaint way.

---

[5] The Strange New World" and "The Rise and Triumph of the modern SELF"

As other faiths have different epistemology than Islam, his work requires an Islamic modification.

Lastly, there are traditional Muslims who possess a deep understanding of sexuality from both Islāmic, modern, and postmodern perspectives, and have written and taught about this topic. I have personally benefited from their knowledge and would like to acknowledge the contributions of Ustādh Mobeen Vaid and Dr. Carl Sharif El-Tobgui. Additionally, two scholars who have greatly aided me in comprehending the differences between the worldviews of postmodern philosophers and Prophets are Dr. Israr Ahmed and Dr. Hatem Al-Haj. In this book, InshāAllāh, I plan to incorporate their work and cover the topic of sexuality from religious, philosophical, communal, socio-political, and jurisprudential angles. I hope that this book can serve as a guide for each and every individual, particularly Muslims living in the West.

Finally, I want to note that this book aims to address the underlying attitudes and ideas that have come to shape modern society's understanding of sexuality, particularly within the context of Islam and the postmodernist paradigm. While our primary focus is on postmodernism, it is essential to acknowledge that these issues have been influenced by many earlier pre-postmodern movements, such as the Enlightenment or the Scientific Revolution. These historical moments contributed to the reduction of human beings to our physical and material selves, which in turn laid the groundwork for the postmodernist perspective. By engaging with these ideas, we hope to provide a comprehensive understanding of the complex interplay between Islamic values and the prevailing Western "orthodoxy" on matters of morality, meaning, and purpose.

Therefore, after asking Allāh for His help, I decided to write this small book. I ask Allāh to accept my efforts. I am starting to write this preface from the Prophet's (صلى الله عليه وسلم) city of Medina. I hope and pray that Allāh protect us all and our progeny from this modern-day trial. Ameen.

Chapter 1: Islām vs Postmodernism

Before we can understand the distinction between Islām & Postmodernism, it would be helpful for our beloved reader to understand the fundamental difference between Modernism and Postmodernism at a simple level, so that we can understand this entire discussion fully. I would also like to add that after the Enlightenment in Europe, a whole swath of philosophies were born: liberalism, conservatism, socialism, Marxism, Neo-Marxism (i.e. "woke" mentality), etc. However, as this is not a book on philosophy, we will not cover all of them. Instead, we will only cover Modernism[6] and Postmodernism, as they are directly involved in the Western sexual paradigm that is the central focus of this book.

Modernism vs Postmodernism from Islamic lens:

A) Postmodernism emerged as a response to modernism around late 20th century, According to Islāmic beliefs, both of these philosophies disregard the divine and traditional moral and ethical values, making them problematic from a spiritual or Islāmic standpoint.

B) The main distinction lies in the fact that modernism originated from Christianity during the Post-Renaissance/Post-Enlightenment era, emphasizing the use of human reason to

[6] Modernism (in the context of philosophy) is a term that was developed in the West to explain the world order that was being established after the Enlightenment. As a result, the Modern Era can be considered as the post-Enlightenment era. To learn further about these topics, the book written by Stephen White titled "Political Theory and Postmodernism" is a good resource. In it, Modernism as a philosophy is discussed in a lot more detail. The book also covers how Modernism links to reason, individualism, liberalism, capitalism, and other philosophies as it constitutes the heart of Modern philosophy. (White, Political Theory and Postmodernism. Cambridge University Press, 1991, page 3

interpret the world without considering faith. Conversely, postmodernism emerged as a response to modernism by challenging both faith and reason.[7]

C) Postmodernism asserts that there is no objective truth, no essence, natural disposition[8], and no objective meaning in life (aspects of Nihilism). 'Reason'[9] is speculative and 'no reason' is definite, therefore no morality is objective, and every morality, whether from text or reason, will be speculative. Hence, the entire focus is on feelings, desires, and personal perception.[10]

D) Postmodernism upholds individualism when it comes to "morality". It maintains that each person should determine their own moral values, resulting in subjective and speculative moralities that cannot be imposed on others. This is in contrast to modernism, where ethics and "morality" were established through collective reasoning. By abandoning this, postmodern morality becomes further fluid. It is worth mentioning that postmodernism's stance on individualism is a little strange; when it comes to morality, every individual can decide their own morality, and it will be considered equal (or equally speculative), and cannot be imposed on anyone. But at the same time, when it comes to individual identity, postmodernists will promote race, sex, and class group-isms, instead of individual identity. Similarly, instead of valuing individualism in markets and politics, postmodernism calls for communalism, solidarity, and egalitarian restraints. In contrast, modern thinkers emphasize the individual: seeing the individual as the unit of reality, holding

---

[7] Fish Stanley, Is there a text in this class? Harvard University Press, 1982, page 180

[8] فطرة

[9] عقل

[10] Foucault Michel, Madness and civilization, Translated by Richard Howard. Random, 1965, page 95

that the individual's mind is sovereign, and that the individual is the unit of value. But morality, according to modernists, is decided by collective reason.[11]

E) Postmodernism holds that language, text, and the world around us can be interpreted in numerous ways, thus preventing the imposition of a single interpretation of "truth," "reason," "faith," "morality," and so on. They believe that all such claims to objectivity and truth can be deconstructed.[12]

F) In a postmodern society, there is a call to dismantle all forms of hierarchy. This includes supporting marginalized groups such as women[13], homosexuals, transgender individuals, and the poor, while working towards the abolition of those who hold power and privilege, such as men, heterosexuals, and the wealthy.[14] This aligns with a Marxist philosophy and aims to create equality across all aspects of life, including economics.[15]

A detailed discussion on this topic is beyond the scope of the discussion in this book. Additionally, since both philosophies reject the existence of God and the unseen world (غيب), they are not in line with Islāmic beliefs.[16]

---

[11] Stephen Hicks, Explaining Postmodernism, Scholarly Publishing, Arizona 2004, page 2-12
[12] Fish Stanley, Pragmatism and Literary Theory, Critical Inquiry 11. March 1985, page 445
[13] Mackinnon Catharine, Only Words. Harvard University 1993, page 22
[14] Dworkin Andrea, Intercourse, New York: Free Press 1987, page 63-66
[15] Lentricchia Frank, Criticism, and Social Change, University of Chicago 1983, page 12
[16] Interesting fact: In order to think clearly about a belief or worldview, it must first be defined. Applying this approach to the topic of postmodernism, a clear definition of postmodernism is needed. Though a number of definitions have been suggested for postmodernism, there is no consensus and some thinkers doubt it can be properly defined. It should also be noted that a number of books and articles on postmodernism never get around to properly defining it. However, we tried our level best to gather different beliefs of this postmodern philosophy and

Differences between Islāmic and Postmodern Thoughts

As a post-colonial Muslim, I want to cross the bridge toward modernity whilst preserving my traditional religion. However, the European precedent of losing Christianity while crossing the bridge to modernity in the past few centuries, causes me great anxiety. We will delve more into this concept in the upcoming chapters.

While there are some advantages to modernism, such as technological advancements that offer new opportunities, it is important to recognize the challenges posed by modernism and postmodernism, including their tendency towards Godlessness. They present two different worldviews, and we, as practicing believers, should be able to distinguish between the two.

The basic difference between modernism + postmodernism and Islām is the belief in the 'unseen' in our fundamental beliefs. Both modernism & postmodernism find it quite difficult to believe in things that cannot be proven by empirical or physical sciences.[17] This leads to unseen religious beliefs being denied by the philosophical community, and doubted by the scientific community. I would argue that postmodernism is more dangerous than modernism because they would deny even 'reason', unlike modernism.

In simple words, Postmodernist might argue that rationality, reason, truth and empirical reasoning, etc. are too laden with a bias to be of any use, at least at face value, and that "Islam" is really what anyone says it

---

presented them to our beloved readers. Please See: Stewart E. Kelly, Understanding Postmodernism: A Christian perspective, IVP Academic 2017, pages 1-15

[17] Whereas modernity can be characterized as a rooting of morality/ beliefs in empiricism, e.g., Darwinian ethics, postmodernity is a rejection of empiricism for this purpose, e.g., subjective morality & beliefs in the occult.

is, that all claims to it are equal, that it has no "essential" content, etc. The postmodern scholarship is used by some figures for similar aims – i.e., debunking traditional orthodox understandings of Islam, thereby opening up space for liberal modernity in the Muslim world.

Three major differences stem from this denial of the unseen world. To understand the difference between Islām and the postmodern worldview, you need to understand each of these differences.

A) Materialism (Body) vs Soul

B) This World vs Hereafter

C) Self vs God

A) Materialism (Body) vs Soul:

Postmodernity believes in the physical/materialistic body but does not believe in the soul, which is from the unseen world. The materialistic body can be proven through empirical sciences as well as through observations in physics, but the soul cannot be observed, seen, or proven via those same sciences. As a result, postmodernity affirms, and consequently focuses on, fulfilling bodily desires and pleasures, while disregarding any discussion on nourishing the soul.

As mentioned, postmodernity finds it hard to believe in the soul, not only because it is from the unseen world, but also because the soul comes from God (All-Mighty), as we Muslims believe.[18] In a postmodern world, people want to disconnect themselves from any higher moral authority (i.e., God).[19]

---

[18] Allāh says ونفخت فيه (I blew my spirit in to human being)

[19] As we will see very soon in the next few chapters, a modern mindset is raised in the environment of abolishing anything that comes from God and tradition.

Once the soul is denied, then there is no meaning or higher objective left in life, because the soul comes with a higher moral authority which the postmodern world rejects. As Muslims, we believe that the soul comes from Allāh, and that without the soul, the body is just a piece of flesh.

If someone today were to ask the question, "Who am I?", the response that might frequently be given would be along the lines of: "You are a mixture of various chemical compounds like water, calcium, salt, etc.". But when one asks themselves who they are, they are not asking about the chemical composition which makes up our physical bodies. How do you define yourself? Are we simply comprised of flesh like other beings? Or do we have something else which differentiates us from the trees outside our house? Something that differentiates us from the computers we use? From the Islāmic angle, we have a body (which is created by Allāh of certain materials) and a soul (created by Allāh, and already aware of His existence).[20]

Synthesis of body and soul through Islām: We can't ignore the soul while nourishing our bodies as we see in this postmodern world. At the same time, we can't ignore the body in nourishing the soul, as the results of this are visible through the failure of certain Christian denominations (i.e., monasticism). Only Islām provides a balance between bodily desires and nourishment of the soul. At the same time, however, the soul has priority over the body, as it is everlasting, and this is why Islām forbade the idea of monasticism.[21]

In short, denying the soul means two things: it is to deny the relationship between human beings and Allāh, and it is to deny the

[20] Al-Quran, Surah Al-A'raf, Verse 173

[21] Prophet Mohammad (PBUH) said: "There is no monasticism in Islām" - Sunan Abu Dawood

meaning of life. It is a recipe that leads to a meaningless life, just like nihilism does.

Since modernism & postmodernism deny the existence of the soul, our materialistic/bodily pleasures are bound to become the purpose of our lives, without any interference from moral laws coming from any higher authority. To add to this, we won't have any higher meaning in our lives, and we will seek whatever way is best to fulfill those bodily/materialistic desires. That is how modernism and postmodernism have led to living meaningless lives in this society.

B) This World vs Hereafter

The second major difference is that postmodernists believe in this world, but not in the hereafter. They not only deny the hereafter because it is from the unseen world, but they also deny the hereafter because this denial removes the sense of accountability and burden of responsibility upon them. As a result, whatever decision one makes, one will not have to consider any of the consequences of the hereafter (i.e. going to Heaven or Hell). Denial of the hereafter also means that their entire focus and purpose in life will be about this world and how to achieve the materialistic desires within it.

To postmodernists, success is defined by materialistic achievements, and failure is determined by the lack thereof. This is very different from the Muslim paradigm of success, and how we think about not only this world, but the hereafter as well. Allāh says in the Quran:

"Every soul will taste death, and you will only be given your [full] compensation on the Day of Resurrection. So, he who is drawn away from the Fire and admitted to Paradise has attained [his desire]. And what is the life of this world except for the enjoyment of delusion."[22]

The Qur`ān teaches us to believe in the Dunya (this world) as well as in the hereafter, and that real success or failure will come in the hereafter as a result of our obedience or disobedience to God in this world, respectively.

Based on the current situation, if the Pharaoh during the time of Mūsa AS (also known to be the biggest oppressor in history) was alive in our times, he would have had a YouTube channel influencing our youth with captions such as: "How to be rich and successful like myself, the Pharaoh". The influence of wealth would cause our youth living in this postmodern world to be starstruck to the point where they would love to take selfies with him. Simply because that is the only way we define success and failure now, simply by the abundance of materials.

Once you realize that the entire postmodern civilization is based on the denial of the hereafter, you will not see the consequences of the hereafter being considered whilst making laws and passing bills. This is regardless of whether the bill is regarding morality, sexuality, or anything else in the Senate or Congress. The entire environment is oriented around the denial of a hereafter, from Netflix to academia, from social sciences in college campuses, to economics and politics. Everyone has lost this sense of accountability derived from the hereafter, and can eventually lead to lawlessness.

Synthesis of this world and the hereafter in Islām: Islām does not ask us to only pursue happiness in the hereafter by ignoring this world and living a life of monasticism, like some of the other

[22] Surah Al-Imran, Verse 185

religions. Rather, Islām forbids a life of monasticism, as evil wants good to perish, and falsehood wants the truth to live in isolation. We, as God-believing people, are asked to engage in the world so that we can make this world a better place. One free from all oppression. Our priority and intention should be to seek Paradise in the hereafter, with the establishment of justice being a means of doing so. This approach brings about a beautiful balance in our belief system.

C) Self vs Allāh

The third major difference between Islām and postmodernism is that the postmodern world believes in the 'self'/human being, but it does not believe in the existence of Allāh. This again stems from its skepticism and denial of the unseen world. Since believing in Allāh is from the unseen, and postmodernism rejects the idea of the unseen, there is a domino effect which results in a few things:

1. They have denied whatever guidance and laws are coming from Allāh. Once you deny the higher authority, why would you believe in the guidance coming from that authority?

2. It means that there is no question about submitting to a higher authority, which consequently means that the 'self' becomes the highest authority.

3. Their thinking process will be human-centric (or honestly speaking, ego-centric) instead of God-centric.

4. They will focus more on themselves instead of Allāh, which allows the entire discussion of the 'self' to follow. This makes finding one's true, authentic self the most important task to them.

5. They will become selfish since the concept of God gives you the concept of family, as well as the concept of submitting to His laws for the greater good.

6. Lastly, the denial of God means there is no objective truth or morality. Everything is subjective, including the word "truth", because every 'self' will have its own 'truth', and this is the essence of postmodernism. In the words of Ryan T. Anderson, "How the person became self, the self-became sexualized, and sex became politicized can be easily understood in our times".[23]

This emphasis on the self means that the postmodern self is not accountable to any higher power, and there is no grounding for their morals or actions. It is worth considering what this 'self' that postmodernists worship in place of Allāh truly is.

Postmodern 'Self' and the Role of Feelings

In the past, if someone went to a therapist and said, "I feel like a woman trapped in a man's body", the therapist would have likely suggested treatments to help align their thoughts and feelings with their biological reality, since how you feel could never change the truth and the reality of your biological gender. However, in today's postmodern world[24], a therapist might instead suggest altering the person's physical body to match their self-identified gender, because the focus is on affirming the individual's feelings of 'self', rather than seeking alignment with objective reality.

---

[23] For more Details, Pls read: - Dr. Israr Ahmed, Islāmic Renaissance - The real task Ahead & Shaykh Abdul Aziz At-Tarifi - العقلية الليبرالية في رصف العقل ووصف النقل & Dr. Carl Truman, Strange New World, Page 12

[24] In the Postmodern world: "truth" and "reality" both are considered speculative. Michel Foucault said: "It is meaningless to speak in the name of-or-against-Reason, Truth, or knowledge", Hicks, Explaining Postmodernism, page 2

If doctors or therapists were to treat patients with gender dysphoria by diagnosing and addressing the underlying psychological issues, as they did in the past, they could potentially face legal consequences in today's society. This is a direct result of the removal of God from discussions surrounding sexuality and gender.

Some Doctors and therapists may argue that psychological convictions and feelings should be given normative authority over the body. However, it should be noted that this perspective is not scientific because:

a) Although science can study both the mind and the body, the relationship between the two, and which one should have authority in the event of a conflict, is a metaphysical issue. This issue is of a more religious nature for believers, and is a philosophical matter for atheists.

b) For individuals who rely on psychological arguments to validate their emotions in order to surpass biological evidence, the fundamental question arises: Who has the ultimate authority to determine whether psychology should supersede biology or vice versa? This highlights the need for objective truth/divine guidance.

When the concept of God as the highest authority is eliminated, individuals may end up worshiping themselves. In the Qur`ān, Allāh says:

أفرأيت من أتخذ إلهه هوى

"Have you seen a person who worships himself?"[25]

[25] Sūrah Al-Jāthiya, āyah 23

In conclusion, the postmodern 'self' that emerges after the removal of God is composed of three key components:

A. The belief that I have authority over my inner feelings

B. The idea that I can only be authentic if I express my inner feelings openly

C. The notion is that society must confirm and validate my feelings and behavior based on my emotions, as I am not submitting to Allāh, and therefore, require people to submit to *my* will

It is evident today that this concept of expressive individualism has become entirely Godless[26].

It is quite apparent in today's society that there is a growing social sensitivity toward criticizing individuals for their personal choices. Any attempt to express disapproval is not only seen as a critique of a certain behavior, but is also perceived as an attack on that person's right to self-expression. This phenomenon is precisely what postmodernism represents - a paradigm shift that prioritizes individual feelings over revelation and reason, thereby granting centrality and authority to subjective experiences.

Postmodern Worldview vs Islāmic Worldview – An Example of Language

How do we as Muslims, who believe in Allāh, His divine guidance, the Day of Judgment, and the concept of reward and punishment, experience confusion regarding this topic? This is because we carry two distinct worldviews within us, and at times, we may not even be aware

---

[26] For more details on the term "expressive individualism", see Robert N.Bellah et al., Habits of the Heart: Individualism and commitment in American life, page 333-334

of them. On the one hand, we have the Islāmic worldview, while on the other hand, we are exposed to the dominant postmodern worldview that is often the default for many. This duality can be better understood through language:

A) Mother tongue and the role of the environment:

How do children acquire language? Is it through studying grammar or by simply imitating the language spoken around them? It is commonly understood that a child's first, or mother, language is solely determined by the language they are exposed to during their early years. Similarly, present day post-colonial Muslims tend to adopt a postmodern perspective, because it is the dominant worldview that surrounds them. The ubiquity of postmodernity in our daily lives, from school and friends, to Western environments, academia, entertainment, government, and commerce, means that we are all inevitably influenced by it, whether we are aware of it or not. As a result, we may be unconsciously 'trained', 'brainwashed', or 'indoctrinated' by postmodernism.

As an example, residing in the United States, English is the predominant language. If I want my children to be fluent in another language, such as Arabic or Urdu, I must teach them separately. However, since they are not surrounded by those languages, the probability of learning them on their own is low, if existent at all. Yet, even if I do not teach them English, they will eventually acquire it, as it is the default and prevailing language in American society.

A similar comparison can be made between the two worldviews. However, unlike language, we will be held accountable for the impact of our worldviews in the sight of Allāh. Thus, we must recognize the effects of these worldviews on us.

B) The majority of us are bilingual, right?

Like bilingual individuals who speak multiple languages, their dominant language is the one they practice and speak regularly and is more likely to be passed down to their children. Similarly, the worldview that one practices and exposes themselves to the most, will become the more dominant of their worldviews. Hence, it is crucial to evaluate which worldview dominates your heart: Islām or Postmodernism?

C) We code switch in our conversations:

As bilinguals, we often mix words from other languages when speaking in English. Similarly, in our worldview, we may "code-switch" between Islām and postmodernism. While some aspects of our thinking and behavior may align with Islām, others may reflect a postmodernist approach, which can be dangerous as it conflicts with Islāmic principles and may lead to godlessness. For example, while a Muslim may immediately label liquor or pork as prohibited, they may adopt a postmodernist perspective on issues of morality or ḥijāb:

"Ḥijāb is just the ḥijāb of the heart and nothing more," or

"Instead of controlling other people, everyone should control their gaze," or

"We should have a free society where everyone is free to wear whatever they want and we shouldn't criticize or judge anyone".

It is important to be aware of the dominant worldview in our thinking and actions, to ensure that we align with Islāmic principles.

How Modernity Came as a Reactionary Response to Christianity

For starters, there might not be any one definite answer to this, just like you can't really blame a ball for shattering a glass window that was already cracked. But certainly, the ball had a significant impact. Similarly, in no way are we saying that Christianity is the only reason why modernity came to be, and the reason for how we think the way we do. But by looking at history, instances like the Renaissance, Enlightenment, Reformation, as well as a few other big players: cultural domination of the West, Imperialism, and Globalization, we can see how expansion of this postmodern thought process came about.

It is hard to state exactly where it all started. How Christianity, which was once taught by Jesus (peace be upon him), slowly but gradually paved the way for modernism. According to my brief analysis, Paul (who died in 64 AD)[27] was certainly a significant figure in this regard. Even though Jesus (peace be upon him) clarified, "Don't think that I have come to abolish (divine) Law"[28], Paul abrogated the entire law, particularly moral law[29] , and consequently, fabricated many new concepts[30], details of which are beyond the scope of this book.[31]

---

[27] St. Paul the Apostle, original name Saul of Tarsus, often considered to be the most important person after Jesus in the history of Christianity. He had a big influence on Christianity as out of the 27 books in the New Testament, 13 are attributed to Paul.
https://www.britannica.com/biography/Saint-Paul-the-Apostle

[28] Mathews 5:17

[29] Read book of Galatians specially Chapter 2, Verses 16-21, Chapter 3 Verses 10-13 and Chapter 5 Verses 1-5

[30] Sanders, E.P.. "St. Paul the Apostle". *Encyclopedia Britannica*, 5 Jan. 2023,

[31] "All early Christians, including Paul, had been Jewish; and the common belief was that Christianity was a new, reformed form of Judaism, Paul transformed Christianity into a missionary religion. He amended and fabricated many concepts which we have in modern day Christianity so much so that his own student Luke said in his book of "Acts" that in Paul's lifetime he couldn't benefit directly from Jesus and when he fabricated new concepts in the original religion then the Disciples of Jesus tried to prevent him." Galatians, Chapter 2, Verse 13

What did the abrogation of law do?

On one hand, it resulted in the Pope filling the void of legislation by making laws, which essentially founded a new religion. Paulism spread completely and took over the entire Christian world.

Long story short, there were many factors that would result in the creation of the Reformation thought process. Factors included the abuse of religious authority in the Church by declaring that whatever the Pope says would be permissible & prohibited, the infallibility of the Pope, several instances of social, moral, sexual and financial corruption[32], as well as the discouraging of learning science,[33] logic, wisdom, critical thinking[34] & philosophy[35] , etc.

In 529 AD the Christian emperor Justinian I, ruling the Eastern Empire from Constantinople, held the belief that Greek philosophy was "inherently subversive of Christian belief," and subsequently closed and banned all the pagan schools of philosophy.[36] This was how philosophy lost its foot hold in Europe early on.

W. T. Jones, the 20th century's leading historian of philosophy, succinctly captured the essence of the decline of Europe, and Christianity's causal

---

& Millman, History of Christianity, Vol 1, Page 377 & Dumellow, Commentary on the Holy Bible, P.L. xxxlx. For more details: Book of Acts, Chapter 21

[32] Will Durant, The Reformation. New York, Simon and Schuster, 1980. page 17-25

[33] W. T. Jones, A History of Western Philosophy, vol. 2, The Medieval Mind (New York: Harcourt, Brace, Jovanovich, 1969), pp. 72–138

[34] Malcolm Lambert, Medieval Heresy: Popular Movements from the Gregorian Reform to the Reformation (Malden, MA.: Blackwell Publishing, 2002), pp. 3–8.

[35] Andrew Coulson, *Market Education: The Untold History* (New Brunswick: Transaction Publishers, 1999), pp. 58–60. Also read: Richard Rubenstein, *Aristotle's Children: How Christians, Muslims and Jews Rediscovered Ancient Wisdom and Illuminated the Middle Ages* (New York: Harcourt, Inc., 2003), pp. 61–62.

[36] Will Durant, *The Story of Civilization,* vol. 4, *The Age of Faith* (New York: Simon & Schuster, 1950), p. 123.

role in promoting it, when he stated: "Because of the indifference and downright hostility of the Christians, almost the whole body of ancient literature and learning was lost. This, then, was truly a 'dark' age."[37]

Seemingly as a result of the loss of philosophy, Dutch economist Angus Maddison confirms that Europe suffered through zero economic growth from 500 AD to 1500 AD (the Dark Ages), which shows that for a millennium there was no rise in per capita income. Not surprisingly, per capita living standards showed no dramatic increases until the Enlightenment.[38]

The Renaissance, roughly starting around the 15th century and onwards (i.e., just after the aforementioned Dark Ages), marked a time of cultural, intellectual, and scientific advancement. From European discoveries of new shipping routes, to new views of science, to the advent of the printing press, the period of "rebirth" following the Dark Ages in Europe was marked by changing ideas, enduring masterpieces of architecture, art, literature, and a movement towards political and "religious freedom"[39]. The shift towards political and religious freedom, in turn, caused a divide within the powerful Catholic Church: the birth of Protestantism. This new sect, and the large number of Europeans who

---

[37] W. T. Jones, A History of Western Philosophy, vol. 2, The Medieval Mind (New York: Harcourt, Brace, Jovanovich, 1969), pp. 139–142. Richard Rubenstein, Aristotle's Children: How Christians, Muslims and Jews Rediscovered Ancient Wisdom and Illuminated the Middle Ages (New York: Harcourt, Inc., 2003), pp. 59, 61–62. Charles Freeman, The Closing of the Western Mind: The Rise of Faith and the Fall of Reason (New York: Vintage Books, 2005), pp. 268–269.
[38] Angus Maddison, Phases of Capitalist Development (New York: Oxford University Press, 1982), pp. 4–7. Angus Maddison, The World Economy: A Millennial Perspective (Paris: Organization for Economic Cooperation and Development, 2001), p.1. Andrew Bernstein, The Capitalist Manifesto: The Historic, Economic and Philosophic Case for Laissez-Faire (Lanham, Md.: 2005), pp. 73–136.
[39] Or Freedom from religious abuse and theocracy which they have witnessed for many centuries.

adopted it, spawned the Reformation movement[40]. This resulted in a bloodbath and a series of wars between different denominations of Christianity from the 16th to 18th centuries, in which millions of lives were lost.[41]

If you connect the dots correctly, you can see that there was not only have abuse, bloodshed, and the Dark Ages due to religious authority and subsequent theocracy, but also the discouraging against learning science & philosophy. On the other hand, the 18th and 19th centuries witnessed the industrial and technological revolutions in Europe only after Europe was no longer being legally suppressed by the Church. Naturally, this places the blame almost entirely with Christianity, and results in a near allergic attitude towards religion in general, particularly in the collective social, economic, and political spheres.[42] This series of historical events confirmed for people that the farther away they were from Christianity, the more scientific advancements they could make.[43] Post-war Europe was the scene of two remarkable changes in religion: secularization (the decline of traditional religion after witnessing the consequences of

---

[40] It's worth mentioning here that during the Renaissance and Reformation, European scholars and thinkers rediscovered the works of Ibn Rushd (Averroes) which had been preserved and translated into Latin by Muslim scholars in the Islāmic Golden age while Europe was still struggling with Dark ages. These works helped to spark a renewed interest in Greek and Roman Philosophy and literature, which, in turn, had a significant impact on the development of modern western culture and that helped lay the foundation for many of the achievements of the Renaissance and Reformation.
For more details read: Britannica, The Editors of Encyclopedia. "Latin Averroism". *Encyclopedia Britannica*, 28 Apr. 2009, https://www.britannica.com/topic/Latin-Averroism. Accessed 14 March 2023.

[41] Will Durant, The Story of Civilization, vol. 4, The Age of Faith (New York: Simon & Schuster, 1950), pp. 769–776. Charles Freeman, The Closing of the Western Mind: The Rise of Faith and the Fall of Reason (New York: Vintage Books, 2005), p. 296.

[42] Peter Gay, The Enlightenment: An Interpretation, 2 vols. (New York: Knopf, 1966, 1969). Andrew Bernstein, The Capitalist Manifesto: The Historic, Economic and Philosophic Case for Laissez-Faire (Lanham, Md.: 2005), 41–54, 70–72, 73–101.

[43] See Andrew Bernstein, The Capitalist Manifesto: The Historic, Economic and Philosophic Case for Laissez-Faire (Lanham, Md.: 2005), pp. 73–161.

abiding fundamentally by it), and the transformation of traditional religious values.[44]

Church vs State – Divine Morality was Confined to The Four Walls of The Places of Worship

As a result of what was learned from post war Europe, from the 18th century onwards, the West established the idea of the Separation of Church and State. This is the idea that neither politics nor government will interfere in the matters of the Church, nor will the Church interfere in the policy making of the government (at least that's what they claim).

The primary reason for this separation of Church and State was to avoid the centuries of religious wars that had previously embroiled Europe, primarily surrounding Christianity. The split between the Catholic and Protestant branches caused some of the most brutal wars seen in modern history, something that the West was desperate to avoid from happening again.

At first glance, this may seem like a good idea, especially considering the socio-political environment of postwar Europe. But in reality, the separation of Church and State meant that Biblical morality and traditional authority were now restricted entirely to the Church, and that policy makers would no longer consider any traditional higher authority or religion in their decision making regarding social/ethical morality. How then, would public morality be decided? The next few chapters will explore how philosophers who were anti-theist in their worldview, played an integral role in defining everything, including morality, after God was officially removed from the collective life of the West, post-Renaissance and post-Enlightenment. Before looking at those big players, however, the next chapter will be dedicated to the

---

[44] Hans Krippenberg, Changing world religion map. Sacred places, identities, Practices and Politics, (pp 2101-2128)

term "sexual revolution" and its definition, so that we can understand the roles of those 'big' players in providing us with an alternative to divine law and how they sexualized the "self".

Conclusion: We can see that how decline of religion in Europe resulted from a lack of divine guidance in defining morality and ethics, and how (arguably) the worst theocracy in history led to a collective allergy and hatred towards religion. As a result, Europe removed God from the social sciences including morality, sexuality, economics, and even politics. Now God could only be obeyed within the four walls of a Church, and human beings were free make the laws however they wished, typically in order to maximize pleasure and minimize harm[45].[46]

[45] West, Henry R. and Duignan, Brian. "utilitarianism". Encyclopedia Britannica, 19 Oct. 2022.

[46] . How did it get imported to Muslim-majority countries when it was only in Europe? Well, that can be attributed to the cultural dominance of the West, imperialism, and colonialism, and the resulting defeatist mentality. All of which got imported to the Muslim world.

Chapter 2: POSTMODERN SEXUAL REVOLUTION

Introduction

You have to understand that we now live in an age where pedophilia and incest are considered filthy (for now, at least), but homosexuality is not. It no longer carries the social stigma in the West that it used to just a few decades ago, let alone warrant a criminal penalty, as is mentioned in Biblical and Islāmic laws.

Nowadays, sex outside of marriage, or outside of any framework (basically casual/lawless sex), is considered common practice, acceptable, and a social norm in the West.

The fact that the most private act that can take place between two people has become so central to public life, is surely a strange development. From legislation on matters such as gay marriage, to controversy over the sexual orientation of athletes and actors, sexuality is front and center in the public eye. Why is this the case? Why has sex become an identity instead of an action? In the Islāmic or Biblical sense, sex was something we did, but today it is considered part of "who we are". Hence, we now have the ever-expanding letters that make up the LGBTQI+ alliance.

What is the sexual revolution?

The postmodern sexual revolution emerged in the early 1960s with the rise of sexual liberation, and the release of the birth control pill to the public. This revolution normalized "hooking up" (i.e. casual sex), and allowed an individual to express his or her sexuality in whatever way seemed right to that person's feelings.

So, the sexual revolution is not only about the transgression in sex that we witness today (e.g. porn industry), because there has been a litany of shameless images found in ancient artwork, and it doesn't only include the relaxation of moral boundaries, like normative premarital sex or the presence of homosexuality, because there were cases of fornication and sodomy even before.

So what makes this sexual revolution so unique and effective is that it has normalized sexual phenomena such as homosexuality, and shamelessness, and has even come to celebrate them? It's the fact that it centers around identifying yourself with your sexual desires.[47]

In simple language, people used to engage in illicit sexual relations and homosexuality before as well, but the sexual revolution has allowed people to escape the feeling of shame, because there is no definite divine morality according to postmodernists. Therefore, there is no social stigma if you watch porn, or commit fornication, or engage in homosexuality. Instead, if you were to say something to a homosexual friend in a non-confirming tone, it would be considered as bigotry and hate speech, as you weren't affirming their "true authentic self". This is in contrast to pre-postmodern times, where individual would have only "felt" gay, but now they "are" gay. This, in a nutshell, is the postmodern sexual revolution; it simply made your identity based on your sexual feelings and desires. Even if a person never had a sexual encounter, just based on their feelings of same-sex desire, instead of deterring them, you now must affirm that "you *are* gay".

Lastly, according to Wilhelm Reich, the very existence of moral principles surrounding sexuality, indicates that sexual needs are not being met. And in a world where sexual needs are foundational to identity, that means identities are being suppressed or denied. The solution,

[47] Wilhelm Reich, The Sexual Revolution: Toward a self-regulating character structure, trans. Therese Pol, Page 25

therefore, is not to change those principles, or merely loosen them. But rather, it is to abolish them in their entirety.[48]

In summary, the postmodern sexual revolution is:

a) Removing social stigma; you can engage in casual sex because postmodernists will neither consider faith nor reason, rather they consider their feelings as the ultimate and supreme authority (i.e. self-worship)

b) Identifying oneself with sexual desire, which has never happened in the history of our planet

c) Abolishing any morality which suppresses your sexual feelings, because of the presumption that your sexual feelings are your identity

The Conflicting and Hypocritical Nature of The Postmodern Sexual Revolution[49]

Even though the postmodern sexual revolution is about breaking down any morality that goes against one's sexual desires, and (by extension) identity, we still see some limits in sexual behavior, like incest and pedophilia. These limits supposedly limit one's authenticity to their true identity. Despite having to do with sexual desires, both incest and pedophilia are still considered to be inappropriate, both socially and legally.

---

[48] ibid, page 23 & Carl Trueman, Strange New World, Page 85

[49] The Quran says this In Surah An-Nisa, Verse no. 82 that if this Quran-centric morality came from anyone else except God then you will find many conflicts and contradictions because it's man-made. In this Āyah, God is telling us that any man-made guidance / morality will have many conflicts and contradictions hence we see the same thing is exhibited in Modern and Postmodern philosophies including how they define morality and sexuality.

The logical question that follows is: what happened to being true to your authentic self and fulfilling your inner desires?

The postmodern world tries to reconcile this faux pas by saying it's not the sex or sexual behavior in incest or pedophilia which is bad, rather it's the issue of consent. Therefore, it is the use of force, coercion and/or abuse which makes them inappropriate.

Do you see what the postmodern world is doing to us?

This is what the sexual revolution has done to us; sexual acts themselves have no intrinsic moral significance in this postmodern world. Rather, it's the consent or lack of consent of those engaging in such practices that now provide the moral framework.

The Logic of Consent:

Since postmodernists place "consent" as an extremely important condition for appropriate sex, it's important for us to talk about this "consent" rule. Just like any other ethical or moral alternative which this postmodern world offers, it is full of inconsistencies, loopholes, and even subjectivity. I intend to demonstrate these deficiencies in the "consent" rule below.

A) Why is pedophilia bad when homosexuality is good?

We know the pedophilia and incest are still illegal in the West, unlike homosexuality. But it seems like it's just a matter of taste more than anything else. Let's apply the postmodern standards for appropriate sex, i.e. the "consent" rule and "no harm principle" to pedophilia and incest.

Postmodernists might argue: pedophilia is bad because it's an abuse by an adult to fulfill their sexual desires without the consent of the abused child. Let's analyze this from the "consent rule" and "no harm principle".

A counter argument for consent would be the way parents make decisions for their children. Parents will force their kids to go to school, and brush their teeth. Sometimes kids will want to eat what's not right for them, and parents have to disregard their lack of consent and send them to school, or discipline them for not brushing their teeth and incorporating good dietary habits. So why does sexual behavior become a unique exception when we define "harm" and "consent", because we see parents going against their kids' consent ALL the time.

Also, regarding the "no harm" argument regarding children, one might say: If one of the parents cheated on his/her spouse, then they have "harmed" their kids because of their uncontrolled sexual desires, which is a relatively common practice in the West. So, we can see "harm" from their particular uncontrolled sexual desires.

B) Why is incest considered bad when homosexuality is good?[50]

Again, it seems that it's a matter of taste as to why incest is still considered inappropriate, while homosexuality is appropriate.

Let's apply the "consent rule" and "no harm principle" to see if they qualify.

In the case of incest, the counter argument against "harm" and "consent" would be: if contraceptives are used to avoid any "harm", while there is "consent" between two adult siblings,

---

50 I just want my beloved reader to know that in Islām, we consider homosexuality, incest and pedophilia absolutely prohibited by all.

then according to the moral standards of the postmodern West, this should be appropriate, no?

A rather sensitive question to ask the postmodernists is: why don't you want siblings or pedophiles to find their true authentic selves?

It's because this issue is just a matter of taste in the postmodern world, where homosexuality is deemed appropriate, and pedophilia and incest are deemed heinous, because clearly, the "consent rule" has too many loopholes.

C) The "consent" rule for extra marital affairs

Bill Clinton and Monica Lewinsky's sexual activity created an uproar in American politics, and was considered to be highly inappropriate, even though both individuals were adults, who engaged in sexual relations willingly and with consent. As she (Monica) wrote: "it was a consensual relationship". So what was the problem with their actions? Bill and Monica were both trying to find their true, authentic selves, and they were both consenting adults.

A few years later, Monica reconsidered her initial statement and said that her relationship with Clinton was full of "Inappropriate abuse of authority and privilege". It was also said that "as an Intern working with the president, her consent might be rendered moot".

Did you notice the loopholes in the "consent rule"? Even if a sexual encounter happened a few decades ago, with proper consent between adults, one can still change "consent" based on one's feelings, because in the postmodern world, one's feelings have supreme authority, as we mentioned at the beginning of the book.[51]

D) Why is Polygamy considered bad when Homosexuality is good?

Let's look at the issue of polygamy: when a man who is already married to one wife, wants to marry another woman with her consent. Both are adults, protecting and preserving the rights of each other, hence there is no "harm" involved. Why then, is polygamy prohibited in the West, when the only standards are "consent" and "no harm"?

This goes to show that this postmodern sexual revolution has certain loopholes, a lack of tolerance, and narrowmindedness for a consenting polygamous arrangement. This also demonstrates that the Postmodern world, which denies faith and reason altogether, has no moral source. But we see that with some basic issues of morality, postmodernism will borrow the morality of Christianity, which is highly monogamous. Thus, postmodernism's aversion to polygamy seems to be a carryover that they've imported from Christianity. Add to the fact that the West has a general allergy to Islām and we see why they would never accept anything related to polygamy, even though it fulfills their criteria of "consent" and "no harm".

[51]https://www.usatoday.com/story/news/politics/onpolitics/2018/02/26/monica-lewinsky-vanity-fair/375452002/

How Modern Technology Helps the Postmodern Sexual Revolution

Modern technological and scientific developments have done two things in helping the postmodern sexual revolution:

A) It made previously implausible sexual behavior, plausible

Contraceptive pills were a huge technological boon for the postmodern sexual revolution. Previously, before the 1960s, Western society was afraid of disconnecting sex with marriage, as any sexual encounter without wedlock could result in pregnancy, subsequent social consequences, and lifelong responsibility.[52] The invention of the birth control pill provided a physical way of making lawless/casual sex safer, allowing it to become more of a recreational thing.

The contraceptive pill's revolutionary breakthrough not only allowed women to separate sex from procreation, but women "on the pill" could control their fertility as well.

B) Technology limited some aspects of nature, which wasn't the case before

Just like artificial rain in the desert, modern farmers don't have to wait for natural rain. Instead, they can use modern irrigation techniques. Similarly, advancements in surgical technology meant that you could entirely remove your capability of becoming pregnant, or causing someone else to become pregnant (i.e. hysterectomy, vasectomy, respectively).

---

[52] Divine morality was already out of equation in Modernity until 1960 but there was a fear of society or morality decided by collective "reason".

There may have been issues initially, as the surgeries were still being developed, but technology made it plausible.[53]

From Philosophy to Action: How the Sexual Revolution Impacted the Daily Lives of People:

1) The contraceptive pill made it cheap and easy to separate sex from reproduction. In short, it made sex a recreational thing, and far more accessible than it had been before.

2) The fluidity of morality led to an increase in shamelessness in mainstream media, leading to the introduction (and eventual normalization) of Playboy magazines and the like, to then porn being presented as glamorous (and also ultimately normalized), and then the promotion of postmodern sexual behavior by Hollywood celebrities as cool and attractive.

3) The increasingly prevalent rhetoric of feminism affirming women's control over their bodies and sexuality over anyone else (including the Creator). Feminists took particular issue with fact that a man can engage in sex for two minutes, and then walk away without much responsibility, whereas the woman has to bear all the responsibility of childbirth and raising a child. Thus, pills and abortion became preferable, and more commonplace, than long term commitment.

4) Mainstream media, including Hollywood, Netflix, and TV shows, etc., all talking about engaging in premarital sex, extra marital sex, homosexuality, etc., without any social stigma. It's now

[53] Rule of thumb: What is technologically plausible shouldn't necessarily be the best option, as most of the technological development these days are human-centric and not God-Centric.

"cool" that you can be true to your authentic self by engaging in abject promiscuity.

This postmodern sexual revolution shapes the way we think about sex, and its world view is very different from the Islāmic worldview, which connects sex exclusively with your spouse.

Chapter 3: The Big players in Revolutionizing Sex – Worshipping "feelings"; the Backbone of Postmodernism

One of the many outcomes of the postmodern sexual revolution, as explained in the previous chapters, is the shift from biology to psychology (or from the body to the mind) when it comes to our sexuality.

One may ask, who grants such authority to the inner feelings or psychological state (especially sexual feelings), that they can trump biology or any outside morality?

There are a few important players who played a vital role in the sexual revolution post-Reformation, and we need to understand them one by one.

Disclaimers:

But before we can start, here are a few important things:

1. **Anti-theism mentality:** All of these players which were integral in giving such authority to feelings, and sexualizing them, actually came after the Reformation, which was when the West was going through an "allergic reaction" towards religion. The West tried to find grounding in their social sciences, which took them to a point where they hated God/religion, or any divine solution for that matter. A verse of the Qur`ān which comes to mind:

ومن لم يجعل الله له نورا فما له من نور

"And he to whom Allāh has not granted light - for him there is no light"[54]

2. **From philosophy to reality**: Most people in the West don't know the names of the big players and influencers in the sexual revolution, like Freud, Rousseau etc. who had a huge impact on constructing the Western worldview. It's akin to how we as Muslims don't pay attention to/bother to remember the narrator of a ḥadīth when quoting or using a ḥadīth. If we think about a fish swimming in a pond, to the fish, the water is simply just the environment it is in; it has never seen anything different, and it has never felt the need to question it. But the scientist who analyzes the water is far more informed about the properties of the pond. Similarly, we live in this environment without questioning the philosophers like Rousseau and Freud, whose philosophies have shaped the modern and postmodern Western worldview.

3. **The balanced Islāmic approach to navigating these feelings – Tazkiyah:** Islām also talks about recognizing and paying attention to our inner feelings. There is an entire science dedicated to it, called Tazkiyah (self-purification or cleansing your heart from evil thoughts), which recognizes inner feelings and tries to bring them in line with divine guidance. But the postmodern world gives so much authority to inner feelings, whilst dismissing any divine intervention, that it ends up identifying individuals by those feelings. And whatever the feelings may be, you need to

[54] Surah An-Noor, Āyah 40

affirm and confirm them, regardless of whether it is beneficial or harmful in the long run.

René Descartes (1596 – 1650) & Jean Jacques Rousseau (1712 – 1778)

René Descartes (1596 – 1650)

René Descartes was a philosopher and a mathematician who came after the fragmentation of the institutional Church during the Reformation. He lived at a time when organic and traditional divine guidance was almost gone, therefore, he tried to follow the path of radical skepticism.

He came to doubt everything, including his existence. The conclusion to his radical skepticism was this phrase: "I think, therefore I am,". So, for Descartes "thinking"[55] had become the ground of certainty.

He published works that posited a distinction between the body and the mind, and his framework gave fundamental importance to the mind over the body, and set the two in opposition.[56]

Descartes didn't know it yet, but his discourse would be integral to the ideas that would make transgenderism plausible in the future.

Jean Jacques Rousseau (1712 – 1778)

Rousseau was a strange but famous man. It was because of him that the "self" became psychologized. His thoughts ultimately became the inspiration for the French revolution.

---

[55] Rene Descartes, Discourse on the method and principles of philosophy, First principle

[56] Rene Descartes, Meditations on First Philosophy, Chapter 2: The nature of the human mind, and how it is better known than the body, trans: John Cottingham, page 20

Motivational speakers and influencers these days use Rousseau's famous statement: "Man is born free, yet he is in chains everywhere".[57]

First of all, this is a very absurd comment from Rousseau. One might respond to it by saying: man is born utterly dependent on others, but in every aspect, he tries to persuade himself that such an obvious fact is not true.

And maybe that is why Rousseau sent five of his kids to an orphanage, because raising kids is a responsibility and it restricts your freedom, hence he escaped that responsibility and "earned" his freedom. Do you now see how this great philosopher defines "freedom"? Did you notice a connection between Rousseau's approach to freedom and the current discourse of "pro-choice"?

Did you detect the denial of Allāh, who gave responsibility to human beings, and will ultimately hold us accountable for those responsibilities? Did you detect the denial about the concept of the hereafter, where we will be punished for our shirked responsibilities?

If you analyze Rousseau's work, you will find two themes:

1) Our inner psychological feelings are actually who we are.[58]

2) Society imposes influence on our inner feelings, which makes us corrupt because we can't be authentic to ourselves until we become according to our feelings or choices.[59]

A few interesting points about Rousseau's impact on the modern western world

---

[57] Rousseau: The Social Contract and other later political writings, pages 41
[58] Jean-Jacques Rousseau, Confessions, Page: 270
[59] Rousseau: The Discourses and Other Early Political Writings, pages 8

1) Child-Centered parenting:

A) Like Rousseau's “self-centered” approach, our Western education system can be characterized as “child-centered”. The West has become so obsessive about actualizing every single feeling (thanks to Rousseau), that it even wants a child’s every feeling to be actualized, lest we don’t allow them to become their “true selves”. So in school, if a teacher tries to discourage any of a child’s feelings, the teacher is seen as the problem, because they are perverting and corrupting that child’s feelings, which is preventing them from becoming their true, authentic selves. Instead, postmodernists demand that society change itself, such that it affirms the inner voice of every child, because doing anything else would be tantamount to inauthenticity. In short, educational institutions in modern day society have gone from being **places of formation, to the places of validation.** Instead of molding the ideology of children in a way that nourishes their souls (in accordance with divine guidance), we’ve had to modify our schools so that they confirm the feelings of children, because doing anything other than that can result in serious legal trouble.[60]

Here is a statement from Reich regarding this child-centered approach:

“The free society will provide ample room and security for the gratification of natural needs. Thus, it will not only not prohibit a love relationship between two adolescents of the opposite sex but will give it all manner of social support. Such a society will not only not prohibit the child’s masturbation but, on the contrary, will probably conclude that any adult who hinders the development of the child’s sexuality should be severely dealt with.”[61]

---

[60] Yuval Levin, A time to build, From Family and community to congress and the campus, how recommitting to our institutions can revive the American dream, page 33-34

[61] Reich, The Sexual revolution, page 23

B) Additionally, if I will only consider myself to be "free" when I behave in accordance with my inner feelings, then all of society is a threat until it affirms me, as exhibited in Rousseau's ideology. So now you will view everyone and every institution from an adversarial lens, until they affirm your inner feelings. Thus, we will begin to exhibit a "what's in it for me" outlook everywhere we go, whether it's the institution of marriage, education, parents, children, etc. This ends up making us more selfish and individualistic. (FYI: we already predicted this outcome from postmodernity, because once you leave God for your "self", then it will make you more selfish (Ego-Centric).

2) Celebrating the Gay Culture:

The celebration of gay culture is a direct manifestation of the adversarial mindset we just discussed. We see it in our own society: when a person comes out of the closet and acts outwardly according to their inner feelings (or when a sister leaves the ḥijāb), and "defies society", they are celebrated. This is because in a postmodern world, my inner feelings are always right, and anyone who says they are wrong (i.e., society) is the "enemy". By going against the "enemy" and acting according to your feelings (i.e., doing what is "right"), you have done something praiseworthy. Anyone who goes against the norms of society will be celebrated as the courageous and brave, adjectives we see being attached to people coming out of the closet all the time. These people are seen as those who are true to themselves, or in other words, are their "Authentic Self".[62]

---

[62] On a side note: That's why the West don't have issues in celebrating "World Hijab Day" because of their oppressor vs oppressed Neo Marxist mentality. Some Muslims get premature excitement about this but we should be cautious for two reasons:

a) They are only celebrating Hijab as a culture. They are definitely not celebrating a Muslim woman surrendering her "choice" and "will" to God by wearing Hijab because they would hate this idea.

3) Anti-Theism:

Some of these philosophers harbor a deep-seated animosity toward religion. This hostility becomes apparent when they claim that society and morality are detrimental to one's true self if they do not align with their emotions. However, in contrast to this, Islāmic law, and other moral and ethical laws, require individuals to regulate their innermost feelings to align with divine guidance.

Karl Marx (1818–1883):

Principles of Karl Marx's ideology:

If you want to analyze the uṣūl/principles of Marx, they are as follows:

A) There is no God (i.e., no moral source).

B) Class warfare: During his time, Karl Marx believed that economic factors are what define our understanding of reality, and informed our identities. He denoted the poor as the Proletarian, and the rich as the Bourgeoisie, and stated that society was about the constant conflict between the two economically (a conflict-based approach). Interestingly, philosophers would later revisit his theory and come up with a theory centering around the conflict between the oppressor vs oppressed, instead of rich vs poor, to continue this conflict-based approach between "classes". They would define the oppressors as male, rich, and heterosexual, and define the oppressed as female, poor, and homosexual. This ideology was called Neo Marxism (which is closely connected to postmodernism).

---

b) When we join them in this oppressed vs oppressor Neo-Marxist / Postmodern paradigm, then they would ask us to join them in Pride month as well which is not possible for any practicing Muslim.

C) Alienation: The idea that a farmer who is working long and hard hours, is barely earning minimum wage and therefore doesn't have the time to become his authentic "self". Therefore, due to economic reasons, he is alienated from becoming his true authentic self.

D) Religion is man-made: Marx not only denied religion, rather he said that religion exists to exploit people financially, and was able to use Christianity in Europe as an example to support his argument.[63] Despite his denial of religion, he stated that there is a need for religion. This need connects back to the idea of alienation, such that a poor man will need religion in order to believe that it is God who is making him poor (not the bourgeoisie/oppressor), so he'll start praying to feel optimistic (instead of revolting).

Marx denied religion so much, that he once said: "Man makes religion, religion doesn't make man. Religion is indeed the self-consciousness and self-esteem of man who has either not yet won through to himself or has already lost himself again. Religion is the opium of the people. Religion should be abolished for people so that they can become happy."[64]

Abolishment of religion:

What ideas can we see in Marx's ideology that could become the foundation for the modern/postmodern West?

A) He states that religion/God/divine guidance are all entirely man-made things which are made to exploit people financially.

[63] Karl Marx and Friedrich Engels, Marx on Religion, page 171
[64] Karl Marx, Marx on religion, page 17

B) He states that the only positive aspect of religion is that it fulfills psychological needs; the pain and suffering that economic alienation causes are alleviated by the false hope offered by religion, where patience will be rewarded and justice will be served. (According to Marx, this is all man-made, but he said it calms people down during times of hardship.)

C) Abolishing religion is important to Marx, because he believed that factory owners/bosses manipulate religion to their own benefit. Religion placates the workers (i.e. poor) so that they bear their present woes, and removes the idea of rebellion; God will bring them out of their troubles eventually. Therefore, debunking religion is vital if the working/labor class is to realize the truly desperate nature of their condition, and then take action to rectify the situation. (Did you detect Anti-Theism, especially in postmodern and neo-Marxist social justice and labor movements?)

In short, Marx lays the groundwork for our contemporary modern West, where religion is a sign of intellectual weakness, and true freedom can be only achieved by the abolishment of religion.

One last thing about Marx, according to him, to bring about true harmony in society, every relationship has to be political. Now do you see why sexuality has become politicized? It's because Marx makes every issue an issue between the rich and the poor, the oppressor and the oppressed. Modern day politics often speak about sexuality as freeing oneself from a tyrannical patriarchy (the oppressor), and not affirming sexual desires as a crime (oppressed). This tells us why school bathroom policies, gender pronouns, and everything in between is a political issue.

Friedrich Nietzsche - (1844–1900)[65]

Like Marx, Nietzsche was also fascinated with the persistence of religious influence. The most famous and ugly statement of Nietzsche was: "Death of God"[66]

What is meant by his "most ugly" statement about God?

Can you see the point where this society officially became Godless, and the need for divine guidance was cut?

Nietzsche picked his words carefully when he said, "God is dead ". To him, it's not that God has naturally become irrelevant, rather Enlightenment philosophy has intentionally denied His relevance and even His existence.

This phrase "death of God " means the death of any moral guidance coming from Him, because when you deny the Creator, the creation won't have any divine guidance or law from the Creator to follow. As a result, morality becomes a tool of manipulation for the strong to exploit and control the weak.[67]

When Nietzsche says his ugly statement "God is dead", it reminds me of a verse from the Holy Qur`ān:

---

[65] This date should remind us that the one who claimed "God is dead" died in 1900 and God is Ever-living.

[66] Friedrich Nietzsche, The Gay science, page 167.

[67] Friedrich Nietzsche, The Gay science, page 181-82

وَلَا تَكُونُوا كَالَّذِينَ نَسُوا اللَّهَ فَأَنْسَاهُمْ أَنْفُسَهُمْ

"And be not like those who forgot God so He caused them to forget themselves"[68]

You might have noticed the hate of religion in the sight of Nietzsche. According to him, for you to be strong, you have to come out of religion, or deny the idea of surrendering to God, and instead of being God's creation, you become whatever works well for you. So what Nietzsche really meant when he said that God (The Creator) is dead, he meant that we are our own masters.[69]

Sigmund Freud (1856–1939):

The single most important figure in the context of sexualizing the self is undoubtedly Sigmund Freud.

He saw sex as the foundation for human personhood and happiness (but civilization requires its containment). You will again observe the absence of divine guidance as they are pursuing ḥappiness from other sources.

From God-centered to Sex-centered life

Freud said in his book:

"Man's discovery that sexual (genital) love afforded him the strongest experiences of satisfaction and in fact provided him with the prototype of all happiness, must have suggested to him that he should continue to seek the satisfaction of happiness in his life along the path of sexual

[68] Sūrat al-Ḥashr, 59:19
[69] Detecting human-centric vs God-centric discourse

relations and that he should make genital eroticism a central point of his life"[70]

Freud was by far the most significant figure in the sexual revolution. According to him, if sex is the strongest factor for human happiness, then sexual desires and feelings should be central to the human identity.

Morality is just a cultural construct to Freud

How does Freud define morality? For Freud, morality is just a cultural creation based on cultural taste to maintain civilization.[71] He considers religion to be childish nonsense, but if it provides some kind of law and order in society, then it's fine to keep around in order to keep society civilized. So, in Freudism, sex is something you "are" and not something you "do", and fulfilling sexual feelings is the most essential thing for human happiness.[72]

Key things:

So far, we have learned from these big players that:

a) Centrality goes from God to human feelings at the time of Rousseau.

b) For Marx, morality is historically conditioned and designed to justify and maintain the current (unjust) economic structure of society and that all religions are man-made.

c) Nietzsche goes so far with his aversion to religion that he says any moral authority is dead, and you should be enslaved to

[70] Sigmund Freud, Civilizations and its discontents," page 56
[71] Sigmund Freud, Civilizations and its discontents, page 56
[72] Sigmund Freud, Three Essays on the Theory of sexuality, page 17-18

your inner feelings without any religious or moral authority from outside.

d) Freud believed that for you to achieve happiness, you need to fulfill your sexual desires, which are the strongest inner feelings (something established before him by Rousseau, Marx, and Nietzsche).

To summarize: the postmodern sexual revolution is all about disconnecting sex from family and reproduction, because the morality coming from divine guidance is very speculative and it is used to suppress the true, inner "self" of people. Also, all religions should be abolished because they are an obstacle to human happiness (which Freud defined as "uncontrolled sex").

Chapter 4: Differences between Islāmic and Postmodern Paradigms of Sexuality:

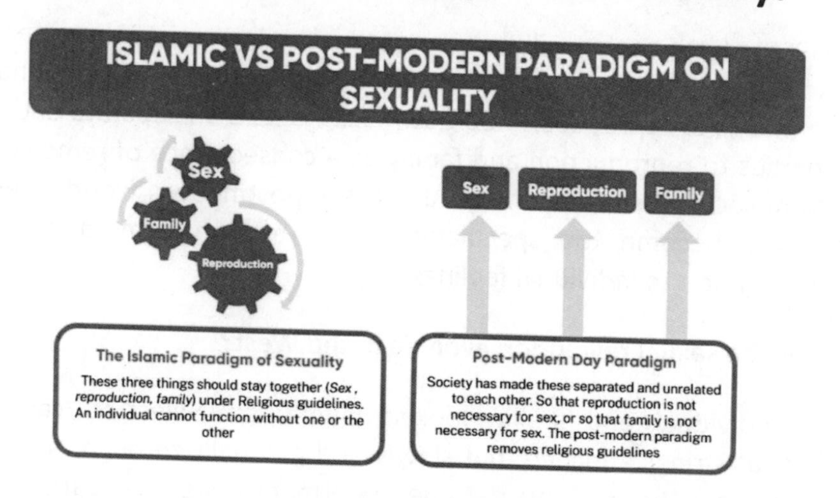

1st Paradigm: Sex, Reproduction, and Marriage

How it started: Before the 1960s, societal norms were aligned with Christianity in the West, and premarital relationships were almost taboo in the US and Europe. Modernity took over post-Renaissance, and the vast majority of people lost interest in religion from a faith perspective. From the social and reason perspective, they were still prevented from lawless sex, as they still gave value to reason. It was a postmodernist mentality that considered every outside morality, whether it's faith, reason, or any other morality, as speculative, and so consequently society focused on individual feelings, and therefore resulted in a disaster.

Paradigm: In Islām, sex, reproduction, marriage, and morality are all tightly bound. This used to be the case in Christianity as well, but in the modern times, they have become separate, free-floating variables.[73]

In 1959, the birth control pill was invented, allowing society the means to disconnect sex and reproduction. Sex became more so recreational than a means to reproduce.[74] So now, "sex" is its own separate entity with no ties to reproduction and family as a consequence of removing God from social life in modernity. And in the postmodern world, even reason has become too speculative for it to define morality, so everything is left to individual feelings.

How has the sexual revolution evolved in the West?

Initially, individuals and families looked down upon lawless sex/casual sex without strings attached, but slowly and gradually through media, immodesty and promiscuity became a normative practice. Early on, what constrained casual sex were biblical teachings, then it was morality and family, then love to a single person, and then consent. Now "consent" is considered the most important thing pertaining to sex, and there is no more moral code or standard that applies to restrict sexual relations.

For Muslims, inappropriate sex is anything outside of marriage, but for the modernist/postmodernist, they have to constantly reinvent the wheel, as they claim freedom, yet they have to continually rework the definition of appropriate vs inappropriate sex. Currently, they say that

---

[73] Even though Muslims are little lenient on birth control or abortion in the early days of pregnancy and they would regard it as permissible if there is a medical need or extreme necessity unlike some Christian denominations.

[74] https://www.pbs.org/wgbh/americanexperience/features/pill-and-sexual-revolution/

sex that incorporates "consent" and the "no harm" principle is considered appropriate.

What are the consequences of following the postmodern paradigm of disconnecting sex from marriage?

a) demise of the nuclear family
b) fatherlessness
c) crimes
d) single motherhood
e) poverty
f) divorces became widespread
g) serial adultery

Now we have a society where kids are more likely to be raised by single parents, two moms, or two dads. Mental health issues are on the rise among kids, so it's no wonder we see chaos in society.

Now, after the postmodern sexual revolution, sex is its own thing after being disconnected from reproduction and marriage. Thereafter, sex was connected with consent (regardless of marriage), youth connected sex with fun, love, romance, and pleasure instead of marriage, and marketers use it to sell their products, implementing the famous principle often seen in Marketing 101 classes: "sex sells".

2nd Paradigm: the Islāmic model of sex + spirituality provides a synthesis between idolizing and demonizing sex

Freudian and Catholics:

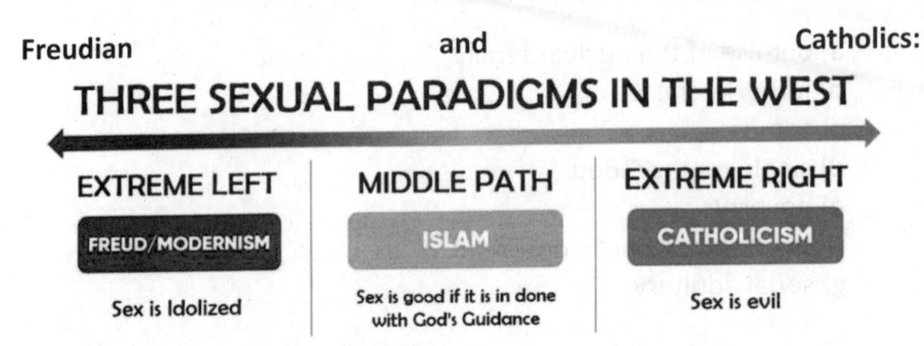

1st Extreme: Catholic worldview

Catholicism sees sex as something of a necessary evil. Saint Augustine, who was influenced heavily by Greek philosophy and Plato's worldview, considered sex as evil because it is from flesh and animalistic characteristics, but at the same time necessary due to its requirement in reproduction.

One thing to note is that Catholicism disconnected sex from spirituality and considered it as something negative, hence St. Augustine advised even married couples to enjoy sex minimally, in order to remain spiritual. This is all visible in the writings of St. Augustine.[75]

Why did Christianity (specifically Catholicism) reach this conclusion? They have such harsh impressions about sex because all of the central figures in Christianity never got married, e.g. Mary (Qur`ānic Maryam), Jesus (Qur`ānic 'Īsa), and John (Qur`ānic Yaḥyā) (Peace be upon them all). All of these figures were never married, and since Christians assign

[75] Saint Augustine, The Confessions, On Sexual Desires, Book 1 & 2 and On Marriage

divinity to some of these figures, they reinterpreted the entire Biblical discourse on sex, as manifested in St. Augustine's writings.

Allāh himself responded to the monasticism adopted by Christians, when He said in Sūrah Ḥadīd:

رهبانية ابتدعوها

"Monasticism is something they invented we didn't prescribe for them[76]"

2nd Extreme: As a reaction to Catholicism, Modern Freudists went to the other extreme

The Freudian movement has idolized sex and made it the purpose of life, and central to their happiness.[77]

They state that sex is something private that doesn't have any connection to God or spirituality, so consequently, they believe that sex and spirituality are disconnected from each other. They argue that God should not interfere in your personal feelings, which is your identity in Freudian ideology, so you can enjoy as much sex as you want because it gives you pleasure. Any outside morality or God doesn't have any right to intervene in your sexual desires. For them, sexual discipline and spirituality are disconnected. Because the entire postmodern liberal paradigm is about maximizing pleasure and minimizing harm, they have already removed God and the Hereafter from their discourse.

---

[76] Surah Al-Hadeed, Āyah 27

[77] Sigmund Freud, Civilization and its discontents, page 56

Islāmic Synthesis:

Islām doesn't see sex as something evil, rather it sees sex as something good, healthy, and part of spirituality, as long as it comes under divine guidance, and is done exclusively with your spouse. That's why wherever you see character development or individual spirituality and morality lessons in the Qur`ān, Allāh brings the discussion of the protection of the privates and satisfying our sexual desires with our spouses only.[78]

Since the postmodern West is based in almost complete sexual laxity, they can't wrap their minds around the Islāmic paradigm of sex: how can the religion of Islām connect sex and spirituality? Because, in their paradigms, sex was never something spiritually positive. Let's go over a few examples of how Islām connects sex with spirituality:

a) In Islām, we remember God All-mighty before every sexual act with our spouse using the words taught to us by our Prophet Muḥammad (صلى الله عليه وسلم):

بسم الله اللهم جنبنا الشيطان، وجنب الشيطان ما رزقتنا

"In the name of Allāh, O Allāh, keep us away from the devil and keep the devil away from what You have provided us."[79]

b) Sex with your spouse is considered an act of charity. Our Prophet Muḥammad (صلى الله عليه وسلم) said:

وفي بُضع أحدكم صدقة ، قالوا : يا رسول الله أيأتي أحدُنا شهوتَه ويكون له فيها أجر ؟ قال : أرأيتم لو وضعها في حرام أكان عليه فيها وزر ؟ فكذلك إذا وضعها في الحلال كان له أجر "

---

78 See Surah Al-Maarij, Āyah 29-31, Surah Al-Mominun, Āyah: 5-7, Surah Al-Furqan, Āyah 68, Surah Al-Isra, Āyah 32

79 Sunan Abu Dawood

"Having intercourse (with one's wife) is a charity." They (the Companions) said, "O Messenger of Allāh, if one of us fulfills his desire, is there reward in that?" He (صلى الله عليه وسلم) said, "Do you not see that if he does it in a ḥarām way he will have the burden of sin? So if he does it in a ḥalāl way, he will have a reward for that."[80]

This indicates that intercourse may be considered an act of worship if the intention behind it is to fulfill the rights of one's wife, to treat her kindly as enjoined by Allāh, to seek a righteous child, to keep oneself or one's wife chaste, to prevent both partners from looking towards or thinking of ḥarām things, and other good intentions.[81]

c) Foreplay is recommended before intercourse, and it is disliked in Islām if you proceed to intercourse without foreplay[82].

d) It is recommended for the husband to make sure that his wife is satisfied sexually.[83]

Could you imagine just how beautifully sex is connected with spirituality in Islām? Islām holds you spiritually accountable if you are not having healthy sex with your spouse. Unfortunately, the postmodern West won't be able to understand this because of the 'privatization' and 'individualization' of sex and religion in their society.

Conclusion: Islām is very restrictive in regard to lawless sex, and we put many restrictions/boundaries on sexual behavior, because we know the consequences of lawless sex on the individual and on the community. But once it's within the boundaries of divine guidance, then Islām

---

[80] Sahih Muslim

[81] Imam Nawwi, Sharh Muslim, 7/92

[82] Al-Munawi, Faidh al-Qadir, 5/115 & al-Tibb al-Nabawi, 183)

[83] Ibn Qudamah, Al-Mughni 9\600 & Musnad al-Firdaws, al-Daylami, 2/55

encourages you to enjoy sexuality, and there's nothing to be ashamed of in doing so.

3rd Paradigm: Feelings, Desires, and Identity

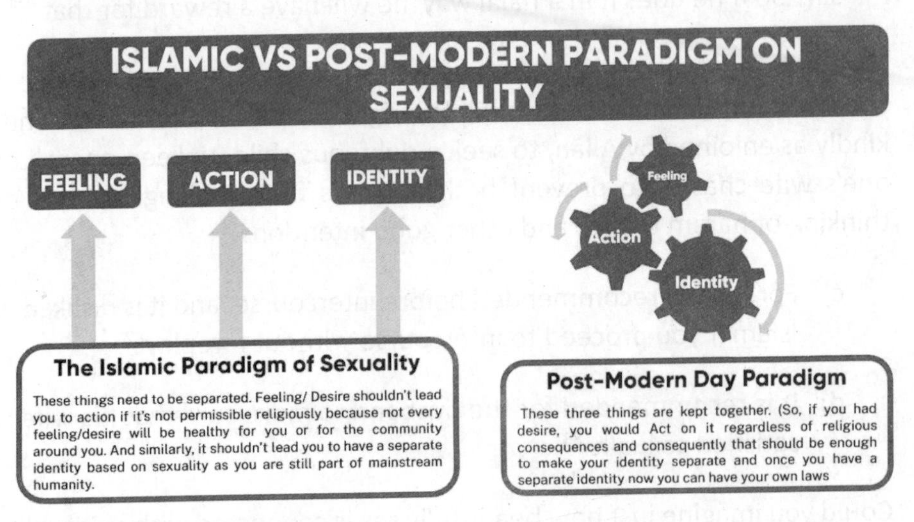

This paradigm demonstrates what postmodernism has done to us; it turned our sexual desires and feelings into our identities. When morality is thrown out of the window, feelings/desires are enough to comprise an identity. Postmodernists disregard every morality, whether it's coming from revelation or reason, because they consider every morality as speculative, and therefore cannot be imposed on others. Consequently, as a postmodernist, you start getting guidance from your feelings/ desires, instead of God.

Never in history have people distinguished themselves with a separate identity based on their sexual desires. Historically, people have engaged in same-sex behavior, like in the Greco/Roman era, and even in Muslim cultures, but never did they brand themselves with that behavior. Today, if a person feels like having anal sex (which is prohibited in Islām) he might say, "I am not just a person, rather I am an 'Anal-sex person', because I feel such a desire and was created that way, so society should accept me as I am. And those individuals/institutions/religions that don't accept me, are all bigots and haters". Some might say that the above analogy doesn't fit current phenomena, and that homosexuality is different. I agree with you; it is different, but that is only because it is being *designed* to feel different. Forces in the postmodern West specifically present same-sex relations in a way that makes them seem natural, and that if you're not on board with the idea, then you are denying reality.

Understanding the identity hoax: If you say fornication is prohibited, some liberals might say that you're outdated or backward, but they still won't say that you are a bigot or a hater, because "fornicator" is never used as an identity.

But if you say something about homosexuality/LGBTQI+, then you immediately become a bigot or hater, because they claim separate identities based on their sexual desires/actions; something that has never happened in the history of our planet. They aim to remove the Islāmic law argument of permissibility/prohibition, by using the identity card and asking you to simply accept their "identity" (and conveniently overlook their actions). They force us to mentally accept their behavior as something normal and natural, and not as a sin or inappropriate, because that behavior is stemming from their "identity".

What's the solution then?

We tell them that your identity comes from your humanity, your religion, your gender (male or female), etc., and that we cannot accept an identity based on your sexuality. We make the case that homosexuality is detrimental for the individual and society at large.

Also, remember that the words we use for our current day personalities were initially words for actions, not for identities. Therefore, you being gay tells me less about your identity, and more so that you commit the act of homosexuality. As Muslims, our identity is something that we *are*, not something that we *feel*.

That's because the moment you accept the identity paradigm of "being gay", it means that you justify their actions at a moral level.

What is the problem with making your desire your identity?

Just the presence of a feeling/desire can never be a moral justification for acting upon it, as some of the feelings in our hearts could be harmful to us or others. For example, if someone desires to cheat on their spouse, just having that feeling does not provide a moral basis for acting upon it. Hence, we must align our feelings to be compatible with divine guidance in order to navigate through them properly.

How politics get involved – sexual orientation and gender identity

Around the world, governments are framing SOGI (sexual orientation and gender identity) laws in relation to the Yogyakarta principle. This is the foundational text in connecting LGBTQI+ rights to human rights.

The 13th principle of the Yogyakarta principles says:

> "understanding sexual orientation to refer to each person's capacity for profound emotional, affectional and sexual attraction to, and intimate and sexual relations with individual of a different gender or the same gender or more than one gender....... Understanding "gender identity" to refer to each person's deeply felt internal and individual experience of gender, which may or may not correspond with the sex assigned at birth, including the personal sense of the body (which may involve if

freely chosen, modification of bodily appearance or function by medical, surgical or other means, and other expressions of gender, including dress, speech, and mannerisms."

We can easily detect three things from this blasphemous principle:

1) The idea of sexual orientation has no objective basis; it is simply defined by subjective desire. It would appear that sexual attraction to anything, a woman, a dog, or a tree, could qualify as a sexual orientation. On top of that, no one can criticize these orientations, lest they be considered a hater or bigot, and even penalized by the law.

2) Gender has been separated from biological sex, and psychology seems to trump biology. A person's feelings have been given moral authority, and if you oppose or challenge them, you will be considered oppressive.

3) Sex is assigned at birth and is distinct from gender. Any judgment by doctors, midwives, or parents will be considered a threat to the child's real identity, which he/she can discover later.

Conclusion: Within hours of President Joe Biden's inauguration, he signed an executive order, "Preventing and combating discrimination based on gender identity or sexual orientation" ... this requires public schools to open women's restrooms and changing rooms to biological men identifying as women. Women's sports, too, must be opened to biological men.[84]

[84]https://www.whitehouse.gov/briefing-room/presidential-actions/2021/01/20/executive-order-preventing-and-combating-discrimination-on-basis-of-gender-identity-or-sexual-orientation/

This means that trans ideology has such a grip on the law, that it will be almost impossible to avoid incident with them if you disagree. Trans rights are now civil rights.

Chapter 5 – Understanding the Coalition of LGBTQI+ in postmodern society

It is important for our beloved readers to know a little bit of the history about the coalition of this movement (LGBTQI+) to understand the current context comprehensively. The coalition of Lesbian, Gay, Bisexual, Trans, Queer, and Intersex people is without a doubt the greatest political success story of the last half-century. The speed, depth, and comprehensive scope of the LGBTQI+ cultural conquest is impressive.

Disagreement within them

Different constituent members are actually divided over the very thing upon which an outsider might assume they are agreed upon: the nature and status of sex. This reminds me of something Allāh says in the Qur`ān:

تحسبهم جميعا وقلوبهم شتا

"you might think they are together but their hearts are divided"[85]

So, what is it that ties them together? Well, this is the manifestation of postmodernism/Neo Marxism as I wrote earlier. In a Marxist society, there is a call to dismantle all forms of hierarchy because of their conflict-based approach between oppressed and oppressor. This includes supporting marginalized groups such as women, homosexuals, and transgender individuals, while working towards the abolition of those who hold power and privilege, such as men and heterosexuals. This aligns with Marxist philosophy and aims to create equality across all aspects of life, including economics.

[85] Sūrah Al-Hashr, Verse 14

So, although there are foundational disagreements betwen them, it's their hatred towards heterosexuals which is tying them together, as the ancient proverb goes: "The enemy of my enemy is my friend".

Disagreement between Gays and Lesbians

Until the early 1980s, lesbians and gay men didn't operate as a united coalition. Lesbians saw gay men enjoying male privilege. Carl Trueman gives the example[86] "The Gay man in the workplace around the 80's was typically not under any pressure to make himself attractive to a female boss to improve his professional prospects. A lesbian, however, might well find that she was required to play a distinctively feminine and sexually attractive role in a heterosexual context for career success. There were also differences in attitudes towards sexual activity itself, Gay men were more focused on genital sex and orgasm, while lesbians were toward affection and companionship."[87]

What Brought the Gays and Lesbians Together? The AIDS Crisis in the 1980s

Because of the AIDS crisis, gay men's image was transformed from privileged middle-class males, to that of tragic victims of a deadly and uncontrollable disease that was closely connected to their sexual identity. As gay men found them increasingly marginalized, like lesbians had always felt, in the 1980s, L and G presented a united coalition focused on presenting a campaign for AIDS research, sex education, and the mainstream acceptance of gay and lesbian people by the wider community.

Three things to learn from this coalition:

---

[86] Carl Trueman, Strange New World, age 129-131

[87] Trueman, Strange new world, page 130

A) There was a shared sense of victimhood in this coalition. Lesbians saw themselves as victims of a heteronormative, patriarchal society, and began to see gay men as victims of the same. This is, in part, a function of the broader culture of expressive individualism that tilts towards seeing virtuous victims: those unable to express outwardly that which they feel inwardly.

B) Both Lesbian and Gay (and even Bisexual) individuals find common ground in their gender and definition as men and women. They both understand the importance of biological sex differences. Lesbians are biological women who are sexually attracted to other biological women. Gay men are biological men who are sexually attracted to other biological men. (bisexuals are those who acknowledge their own biological identity, as well as their sexual attraction to others of either biological identity.)

C) If you followed along closely, you might think the biggest enemy for Lesbians, Gays, and Bisexuals would be some group that separates biological sex from gender, and who denies the traditional categories of male and female in favor of a fluid and ever-changing range of multiple sexual identities. But surprisingly, you would see that Trans and Queer join this coalition, despite denying the common grounding beliefs of Lesbians, Gays and Bisexuals. Lesbian, Gay, and Bi all assume the sex binary of male and female as grounded in basic biology, and that core belief is denied by Trans, as they separate sex from gender.

This addition of the T and the Q to LGB is incoherent. One may ask, why did this happen? Well, as they say: “The enemy of my enemy is my friend”, because whether it’s L, G, B or T, or Q, all of them have a common enemy in a heteronormative society.

Trans ideology and Feminist movements

There are only two genders in the Islāmic paradigm

Before we take a look at the origins of trans ideology, we want to make it very clear from the Islāmic paradigm that there are only two genders, as confirmed by numerous textual evidences,[88] and the agreement of all the scholars[89]. Obviously, the postmodern paradigm of sexuality won't consider any revelation or reason (that's why we are facing such chaos regarding our sexuality in the first place), and as a result, we can't even keep up with the ever-expanding rolodex of genders.

Also, according to the Islāmic paradigm, the two sexes are equally human and equally noble. There is no spiritual superiority of either gender over the other, and both have equal access to divine blessings, grace, forgiveness, and Paradise.

There are simply too many verses in the Qur`ān that refer to the two sexes, for us to deny a fundamental gender binary, and there is no reference whatsoever in the Qur`ān to anything other than this. It is an undeniable reality that numerous Islāmic legal and social rulings differ between males and females. These rulings are found in all legal textbooks, and run from the beginning chapters of purification all the way to the ending chapters of inheritance. Many aspects of our Islāmic

---

[88] Allāh says: "And by his creation of male and female" Surah Al-Layl, 92:3
Allāh says: "And that he created the two mates, the male and the female" Surah An-Najm, 53:45
Allāh says: "And the male is not like a female" Surah Al-Imran, 3:36
[89] Al-Jassas, Ihkaam Ul-Quran, 5]298
Ar-Raazi, Tafsir Al-Kabeer, 31\182
Az-Zamakshari, Al-Kashaf, 4\762
Al-Kasani, Al-Badai' As-Sanai', 7\327

law are inherently gender-based, and one finds different rulings for men and women in almost all chapters of the Islāmic legal system.

The contemporary distinction between biological sex and psychological/cultural gender, might have some elements of truth to it (for example, it is correct that some aspects of traditional gender roles are culture based). However, to claim that "gender" in its entirety is a cultural construct, bearing no essential relationship to biological sex, is simply incorrect. The very DNA of males and females is different. It is precisely because males and females are different—physiologically, biologically, emotionally, and in so many other ways, that Islāmic law clearly delineated the broad outlines of responsibilities of each of the two genders.

Therefore, the contemporary claim that gender is an imaginary or cultural human construct, with no necessary link to biological sex, is untenable in the light of scripture, Islāmic law, biology, common sense, and the cumulative history of mankind.

Someone might ask, what about intersex? Okay, let's discuss intersex.

Intersex is not a separate gender

There are some people known as intersex individuals who are born with ambiguous genitalia, and/or have atypical sex chromosomes. Intersexuality is a relatively rare phenomenon, and is comprised by a number of sub-categories. In fact, in many cases, a person may not even be aware of this phenomenon until undergoing a medical exam.

There are a handful of specific rulings in the books of fiqh under the topic of "khunthā" that deal with the phenomenon of intersex. However, these are specific concessions and rulings for those born with both private organs, which itself is a rarer sub-category of intersex individuals.

It is to be noted that even in such cases, where it's understood that intersex conditions are beyond a person's control, and hence not sinful, still require the intersex person to live his or her life according to the Islāmic rulings of the gender he or she is physically and biologically closest to (typically decided on the basis of the biological functionalities of the sexual organs, and which of the two is predominant). On very rare occasions, including some individuals who are completely sexually androgynous, the Sharī'ah might consider such individuals as being essentially of indeterminate gender for some aspects of life (such as where to stand in prayer in a masjid). In other aspects of this individual's life, however, (such as inheritance), a primary gender will be selected in consultation with religious scholars and medical doctors, and the rulings associated with that selected gender will apply for the remainder of the individual's life for those other aspects. But, it should be loud and clear that even in intersex, the third gender won't be assigned, because there are primarily two genders from the Islāmic perspectives.[90]

Difference between Intersex and Transgender

The term "trans" as it is used in today's culture is a very broad term encompassing many different aspects, and it is a mistake to equate the discussion in the books of Islāmic law on "khunthā" (intersex) as being equivalent to the modern "trans" category. Specifically, as we have seen, the phenomenon of intersex—which is what shar'ī discussions of the khunthā are about—stems from a physiological abnormality that renders the individual's classification as male or female objectively ambiguous. By contrast, current-day transgenderism references a psychological condition, in which the trans individual subjectively "disidentifies" with the gender of the unambiguously male or female body in which he or she was born in.

[90] https://muslimmatters.org/2022/06/21/fatwa-regarding-transgenderism/

Origin of Trans Ideology:

Now let's focus on trans ideology. There are a few origins of trans Ideology that we need to note before we can start this discussion:

a) In the 19th century, automation in the workplace became increasingly more robust, and removed the necessity for the hard, manual labor often done by men. Which meant that the physical difference between men and women would shrink.

b) Nietzsche's anti-metaphysical philosophy, with its stress on how we ourselves have a godlike power to create truth, also lends itself to the denial of stable categories such as male and female.

c) Psychologizing the "self" also opens possibilities for trans ideology. This essentially grants the physical body less authority than the mind in determining identity. The body becomes an instrument, or the raw material, for realizing or expressing identity as determined by the will.

d) Then came the feminist movements, especially Simone De Beauvoir, who came up with the basic idea of the difference between sex and gender. In her book, "The Second Sex", she said: "One is not born but rather becomes, woman. No biological, psychic, or economic destiny defines the figure that the human female takes on in society; it is civilization as a whole that elaborates this intermediary product between the male and the eunuch that is called feminine."[91]

[91] Simone De Beauvior, The Second Sex, Page 257

So basically, the idea of a woman, according to her, is a social construct and something that is not intrinsic to the female body. In short: sex is biologically constructed and gender is socially constructed.

There is partial truth in the idea that a different culture will have different social roles for the genders. The women in Pakistan will have different cultural expectations to the women in New York, but to take it to the next level where you can deny the basic definition of women and biological facts, is insane.

To make the idea of separating sex and gender possible, a few factors must be in play:

A) Inner psychology must have been granted ultimate authority in human identity, and God and divine guidance must be removed.

B) Technology also must be able to support the changing of gender.

C) The existence of a powerful lobby group and an attractive media presence in order to help normalize the idea. (which is what the LGB movement provided to the Trans community)

Beef between Trans and Feminists

Understandably, some feminist thinkers don't like the trans movement. They believe that we need to deny trans women as real women, otherwise they will deny all the male privilege that has been their invisible birthright, and falsely identify with female victimhood. An obvious example is women's sports.[92]

This is why one of the feminist thinkers, Janice Raymond (American Lesbian radical feminist professor), said: “sex and gender are not the same things but biology plays a vital part of being a woman because it shapes how women experience the world. For example, menstruation and pregnancy have huge consequences both financially and physically, which trans women, who are biologically male, can never imagine.” [93]

In the face of the trans phenomenon, a feminist accepts the reality of gender.

Trans Logic

Since divine guidance has been thrown out of the window, the logic upon which the trans ideology depends, is that it assumes that the body is not of primary relevance in determining gender identity. They consequently exclude bodily considerations from the definitions of what it means to be a man or woman.

To summarize, trans ideology gives more importance to psychology than biology in defining gender.

---

[92] Lucy Clarke-Billings, “Germaine Greer in Transgender Rant: 'Just because you lop off your penis, It doesn't make you a woman” Telegraph, October 26,2015, http://www.telegraph.co.uk/

[93] Janice Raymond, Transsexual empire - The making of the she-male, page xx

Chapter 6: Revisiting a Few Postmodern Doctrines in the Context of LGBTQI+

Doctrines:

a) Hate the sin not the sinner

b) Moral policing

c) Social justice

Revisiting the self-imposed doctrine of "hate the sin not the sinner"

The first accusation you will get if you are being critical of the LGBTQI+ movement is of being a bigot/hater. So let's discuss this in a little more detail by summarizing what Shaykh Hatem Al-Haj discussed beautifully in his book "Love and Hate in Islām".

This issue is loaded and surrounded with intense emotions, which cloud an impartial inquiry into the truth. People are ready to label you after reading the preface of your book, or just even a heading. It's difficult to discuss the topic without facing accusations of both laxity and extremism, regardless of where you stand on the spectrum. However, if you choose to align yourself with one end of the continuum, you will only be accused of one of these things. Should traditional scholars avoid discussions altogether? We can't afford that. Not only because we have the obligation to convey the message of Islām, but also because our silence will be extremely consequential. The loss of balance and moderation (وسط) in addressing this issue will lead many to extremism on one side or the other.[94]

---

[94] Dr Hatem, Love and Hate, Revisiting the doctrine of al-Wala' wal-Bara', page 27-100

Revisiting the idea of "hate the sin not the sinner"

I used to say this phrase a lot during my speeches, like some other well-known and respected preachers. But recently, I've felt that this might not be a valid principle for Muslim speakers, activists, or scholars, for a number of reasons. So please see the following.

If "hate the sin not the sinner" is true, then we would ask a father to hate the act of rape, but not the rapist who raped his daughter. Think about it, is this even possible?

Furthermore, for Muslims, there is no definite evidence from our scriptures that reflects this distinction between the act and the actor (i.e., the sin and the sinner). In fact, it's the other way around. The Prophet صلى الله عليه وسلم said: "A fornicator who fornicates is not a believer while he commits fornication…"[95]. There are numerous aḥādīth that say Allāh hates the sinner. Some examples are mentioned below:

A) Whoever does not call upon Allāh, He will hate him[96]

B) The Khawārij (religious extremist) are among the most hated creations of Allāh[97]

C) The most hated amongst people in the sight of Allāh are the ruthless argumentative (people)[98]

D) Allāh hates the profligate and the obscene[99]

---

[95] Bukhari
[96] Sunan Tirmidhi, Hassan
[97] Sahih Muslim
[98] Sunan Tirmidhi, Sahih
[99] Al-Jami' As-Saghir, Sahih

From a legal standpoint, the criminal gets punished for his crime by the court, and the sinner gets punished for his sin by Allāh. So how do we differentiate between the two?

From an Islāmic standpoint, we can consider the following ḥadīth:

مَنْ أَحَبَّ لِلَّهِ وَأَبْغَضَ لِلَّهِ وَأَعْطَى لِلَّهِ وَمَنَعَ لِلَّهِ فَقَدْ اسْتَكْمَلَ الْإِيمَانَ

"Whoever loves for the sake of Allāh, hates for the sake of Allāh, gives for the sake of Allāh, and withholds for the sake of Allāh has perfected the faith"[100]

The ḥadīth is clear about hating someone for the sake of Allāh. How can we reconcile this ḥadīth with the principle of "hate the sin not the sinner"?

Also, to put things in perspective, in recent years, "hate the sin not the sinner" is often revived by Christian denominations in debates about homosexuality and gay marriage.[101]

I also understand that there could be a problem with using the word "hate" in the English language as a translation of بغض, because hate sometimes entails potentially doing harm, like in the phrase "hate crime", and can have negative connotations. But when we are talking about hating a sinner with a "religious hate", it is different from the English connotations. So, we can consider the following points:

100 Al-Jami' As-Saghir, Sahih

101 https://www.usatoday.com/story/news/2017/01/04/kim-burrell-hate-the-sin-love-the-sinner/96158416/

- Religious hate does not allow any harm to be done, as clarified by scholars[102]

- Religious hate also doesn't mean absolute hate, rather it's connected to that sin only; you might love the same person for some other positive aspect.

- Religious hate also means that this kind of hate should come out of love and goodwill, and that we should constantly wish and make du'ā` for the guidance of those people, just like the Prophet صلى الله عليه وسلم made du'ā` for Abu Jahl, the people of Ṭā`if, etc.

Moreover, why would we teach people to hate? Why not teach absolute love?

A. We are not teaching people to harm others with this "religious hate" (as could be misconstrued via the English connotations). Rather, we are asking them to dislike the sinner because that dislike is something uncomfortable. By forcing ourselves to engage in this discomfort, we can avoid sinning ourselves, knowing that others may dislike us as well. The feeling of dislike that we are calling religious hate, is necessary to give us the motivation to avoid sin.[103] With that in mind, arguments like "hate the sin not the sinner" serve to desensitize us, and actually push us towards sin by way of omitting hate of the sinner.

B. Each culture has its own values and standards that predispose its denizens to love or hate certain things. If you go against the social and ethical norms of that society, they will invariably dislike you. For example, if I, as a Muslim father, teach my kids that

---

[102] Shaikh Mohammad Shamsulhaq AlAzeem Abadi, Awn-ul-Mabood fi Sharh Abi Dawood no. 4681.

[103] Carmen Marrick, Hating Evil: Understanding the Role of Evil in Interpersonal Hate

homosexuality is prohibited in Islām, or that gender is biological and binary, then someone from this society might hate me and label me as homophobic or transphobic. Given my Islāmic values and standards, I will hate them for teaching my kid about these things, and I might call them Islāmophobic.

C. In Islām, we are not egocentric but God-centric. We don't hate something because of our own personal disliking, rather whatever God dislikes, we dislike as well.

D. We can't have an absolute love for criminals, rapists, murderers, oppressors, etc. Therefore, we would use the term conditional love rather than absolute love to be realistic/pragmatic.

Finally, I don't know what the replacement for "hate the sin not the sinner" could be; it would have to be something that more closely aligns with Islām. Maybe we can say this, as suggested by Shaykh Hatem Al-Haj:

"Hate of a sin is the hate of a hater, and hate of a sinner is the hate of a lover."[104]

Differentiating between sincere strugglers of homosexuality/transgenderism vs Influencers in our communities

Going back to the paradigm for a minute, we should recognize that if a person is struggling with same-sex desires (regardless of whether he/she acted on those desires), they should be treated like any other heterosexual person who is sincerely struggling with their sexual desires. This recognition comes from morality guidelines found in the Sharī'ah.

[104] Shk Hatem Al-Haj, Love and Hate in Islām, Page 62

As a result, we see them as sincere strugglers, and that Allāh will reward them for their patience with those desires.

If a person is struggling with Gender Dysphoria, but is aware of the Islāmic morality and paradigm of sexuality, or if they have undergone gender altering surgeries and then reverted to Islām, or recognized their mistake and become practicing Muslims, they too should be regarded as sincere strugglers. It is important to deal with them with optimism, love, kindness, and compassion, and to pray that Allāh will grant them the strength to adhere to His legislation.

If you compare the above-mentioned case to a Muslim or non-Muslim, who not only affirms his/her identity as homosexual or transgender, but also influences others as well and is quick to label anyone who tries to give them Islāmic advice as a bigot or hater, then we will have to deal with them with justice, not with compassion. We will make sure that this person does not have any influence or impact on our larger Muslim communities, as this is detrimental to our faith. Having said that, we will still hope and pray that they will stop acting in that manner, and stop influencing others as well.

So now we have to answer a crucial question: how can we make a distinction in Islāmic law between sincere strugglers vs those that legitimize homosexual/transgender feelings?

Well, any basic student of Islāmic sciences will be able to tell you that we deal differently with different non-Muslims. We see that in the case of the Prophet's (صلى الله عليه وسلم) two uncles: Abu Lahab and Abu Ṭālib. Both of them were non-Muslims and died in that state, but the Prophet (صلى الله عليه وسلم) dealt with them in very different ways. The reason for the difference was that Abu Lahab was a vicious enemy to Islām, whereas Abu Ṭālib was a strong supporter of it, yet both of them were non-Muslims. Even Allāh used different language for them in the Qur`ān;

Allāh uses very strong language in Sūrah Lahab. In another case, Allāh uses gentle language. As Allāh says:

إنك لا تهدي من أحببت ولكن الله يهدي من يشاء وهو اعلم بالمهتدين.

"Indeed (O Muḥammad) You do not guide whom you love..."[105]

According to the vast majority of tafsīr scholars, this āyah is talking about Abu Ṭālib. When the āyah says من أحببت (whom you love), it doesn't mean that the Prophet صلى الله عليه وسلم loved the religion of his uncle, rather it means he loved his uncle despite his polytheistic religion, and really wished for him to accept Islām out of that love. In contrast, when it comes to Abu Lahab, Allāh said:

تَبَّتْ يَدَا أَبِي لَهَبٍ وَتَبَّ

"May the hands of Abu Lahab be ruined, and ruined is he[106]"

Similarly, there are numerous verses of fighting and killing non-Muslims like:

"And kill them wherever you find them..."[107]

"Not taking them friends"[108]

How would you reconcile these āyāt with the Islāmic ethos of showing kindness and justice to those who disagree with us in our faith? i.e., non-Muslims[109]

---

[105] Surat Al-Qasas, Āyah 56
[106] Surah Masad, Āyah 1
[107] Surah Al-Baqarah, Āyah 191
[108] (Surah At-Taubah, Āyah 23, Al-Maida, Āyah 51)
[109] (Surah Al-Mumtahanah, Āyah 8)

Who should be connecting the dots and reconciling the apparently conflicting verses and narrations, which talk about fighting with the disbelievers? One of the well-grounded scholars in the tradition, Imām Ibn Taymiyyah, wrote a treatise in which he showed conclusively that the 'illah (legal basis) for fighting them, is their aggression, not their disbelief. Imām Ibn Taymiyyah said that the text implying an open fight against them can never be used as proof for fighting people at large, because they appear to conflict with other evidences.[110] So we can safely say that any non-hostile, non-influencer, "sincere struggler" amongst the homosexual community or transgender communities, regardless of whether they are Muslim or non-Muslim, will not be equal to the hostile, influential individual from those communities.

Etiquettes of dealing with the sincere strugglers amongst homosexuals and transgenders

Let us identify the etiquettes which we should abide by when dealing with sincere strugglers amongst homosexuals and transgenders within the Muslim or non-Muslim community.

A) Kindness: Allāh says:

لَّا يَنْهَاكُمُ اللَّهُ عَنِ الَّذِينَ لَمْ يُقَاتِلُوكُمْ فِي الدِّينِ وَلَمْ يُخْرِجُوكُم مِّن دِيَارِكُمْ أَن تَبَرُّوهُمْ وَتُقْسِطُوا إِلَيْهِمْ ۚ إِنَّ اللَّهَ يُحِبُّ الْمُقْسِطِينَ

" Allāh does not forbid you from those who do not fight you because of religion and do not expel you from your homes - from being righteous toward them and acting justly toward them. Indeed, Allāh loves those who act justly"[111]

[110] Ibn taymiyyah, qitaal al-kuffar wa muhadanatuhum, page: 87-99

[111] Surat Al Mumtahana, Āyah 8

It is noteworthy that in this āyah, the Arabic word for "dealing kindly" is the word "tabarruhum" which is usually used in the context of dealing with one's parents, with whom one is required to show the highest level of benevolence. This is the Qur`ānic āyah most quoted by Muslim scholars with respect to relations with others.[112]

Caution: Having said that, we should not overcompensate in this regard, like some Muslims in the West that have a defeatist mentality. We should not be like Muslims who give more kindness to these people, than to their own practicing brothers and sisters. It will consequently give the wrong message to practicing Muslim youth; our interactions should be done in a balanced and wise way.

B) Justice

Refraining from all forms of injustice is the hallmark of the Islāmic value system, and the bedrock of its theory. Any concept, legal code, or human behavior must be brought into line with this foundational matrix, and find a place within it, otherwise, it is not Islāmic. Interaction with a homosexual or transgender or non-Muslim is not an exception to this rule, because there is no evidence to have such exceptions.

Abdullah ibn Amr (R) narrated from the Prophet (صلى الله عليه وسلم), that he said:

من قتل نفسا معاهدا لم يرح رائحة الجنة

"Whoever killed a mu'āhid (a covenanted non-Muslim) shall not smell the fragrance of Paradise [113]"

[112] Imam Raazi, Mafatih hul-Gayb, 29\521
[113] Al-Bukhari

In another report, the Prophet (صلى الله عليه وسلم) said:

ألا من ظلم معاهدا او انتقصه أو كفله فوق طاقته أو أخذ منه شيا بغير طيب نفس فأنا حجيجه يوم القيامة

"If anyone wrongs a mu'āhid, detracts from his rights, burdens him with more work than he is able to do, or takes something from him without his consent, I will plead for him (the mu'āhid) on the Day of Resurrection"[114]

The Prophet (صلى الله عليه وسلم) also said:

والله لا يؤمن، والله لا يؤمن، والله لا يؤمن، قيل: يا رسول الله ومن؟ قال: الذي لا يأمن جاره بوائقه

"By Allāh, he does not have faith; by Allāh, he does not have faith; by Allāh, he does not have faith." It was asked: O Messenger of Allāh, who is that? He replied: "The one whose neighbor is not safe from his annoyance."[115]

Imām Qurṭubi commented on this ḥadīth in his tafsīr, explaining: "This is general in meaning and applies to all neighbors"[116]

C) Individual accountability:

Since stereotyping is a terrible form of injustice, Allāh teaches us to avoid it. He says,

---

114 Reported by Abu Dâwood; classed as ṣaḥeeḥ by al-Albâni in Ṣaḥeeḥ Abi Dâwood
115 Agreed upon
116 Tafseer Al-Qurtubi, 5:183

وَمِنْ أَهْلِ الْكِتَابِ مَنْ إِن تَأْمَنْهُ بِقِنطَارٍ يُؤَدِّهِ إِلَيْكَ وَمِنْهُم مَّنْ إِن تَأْمَنْهُ بِدِينَارٍ لَّا يُؤَدِّهِ إِلَيْكَ إِلَّا مَا دُمْتَ عَلَيْهِ قَائِمًا ۗ ذَٰلِكَ بِأَنَّهُمْ قَالُوا لَيْسَ عَلَيْنَا فِي الْأُمِّيِّينَ سَبِيلٌ وَيَقُولُونَ عَلَى اللَّهِ الْكَذِبَ وَهُمْ يَعْلَمُونَ

"Among the People of the Book are some who, if entrusted with a hoard of gold, will (readily) pay it back; others, who, if entrusted with a single silver coin, will not repay it unless you constantly stand demanding it, because, they say, "There is no call on us (to keep the faith) with these ignorant (pagans)." But they tell a lie against Allāh, and they know it.[117]

The Prophet صلى الله عليه وسلم promised the Christians of Najrān that none of them would be held accountable for the crimes of another[118].

So, if one homosexual or transgender individual hates Muslims, then it doesn't mean that we should deal with the sincere strugglers in the Muslim community in the same way.

D) Being critical shouldn't come at the expense of respect

The Messenger of Allāh صلى الله عليه وسلم taught us by example to respect everyone's humanity when he stood during the funeral procession of a Jew. He remained standing until the corpse was buried, even though people informed him it was the funeral of a Jew. To that he said:

أليست نفسا؟

"Isn't it a soul?"[119]

[117] Surat Âl 'Imrân, āyah 75
[118] Aḥmad al-Ya'qoobi, "Tareekh al-Ya'qoobi," n.d., 1:138. Accessed July 1, 2021, http://Islāmport.com/w/tkh/Web/364/138.htm
[119] Agreed upon

This is not unexpected of the Messenger صلى الله عليه وسلم, who has also conveyed to us Allāh's statement:

وَلَقَدْ كَرَّمْنَا بَنِي آدَمَ وَحَمَلْنَاهُمْ فِي الْبَرِّ وَالْبَحْرِ وَرَزَقْنَاهُم مِّنَ الطَّيِّبَاتِ وَفَضَّلْنَاهُمْ عَلَىٰ كَثِيرٍ مِّمَّنْ خَلَقْنَا تَفْضِيلًا

"And We have certainly honored the children of Ādam and carried them on the land and sea and provided for them of the good things and preferred them over much of what we have created, with [definite] preference."[120]

How can we not have respect for humans, when Allāh made the angels prostrate before their father (Ādam AS) and He breathed into humans from His spirit?[121]

Caution: At the same time, respecting someone doesn't mean you agree with their wrongdoing/sin, or praise them for their paradigm of sexuality. Be respectfully critical, and remember that this religion requires you to constantly advise your brother/sister who is struggling with any desire, let alone a homosexual or a transgender individual. This will bring balance to your approach when dealing with sincere strugglers in the Muslim community.

E) Sharing life's mundane exchanges

'Ā`ishah (May Allāh be pleased with her) reported that at the time the Messenger of Allāh صلى الله عليه وسلم died, his armor was mortgaged with a Jew for thirty ṣā's (measures) of barley.[122]

It may seem superfluous to include this, however, this is not simply about the permissibility of financial dealings with sinful Muslims or non-

---

[120] Surah Isra, Ayat:70

[121] Al-Hijr 15:29 and Saad 38:72

[122] Agreed upon

Muslims; it is about sharing those human activities across religious backgrounds, without setting up any partitions. It is rather unlikely that the Prophet صلى الله عليه وسلم could not find a single Muslim to get barley from by mortgaging his armor. It also shows us that his fair and pleasant dealings with the Jews in Medīnah lasted until the end of his life. Islamic law considered the testimony of the non-Muslim expert witness like that of the Muslim. [123] Muslim scholars accepted the oath of the non-Muslim in litigation against a Muslim, whether he is the defendant[124] or even the claimant.[125]

From the Sharī'ah standpoint, I can't find any evidence which says that engaging in business transactions with sincere strugglers amongst homosexuals or transgenders is ḥarām. So, we will go with the Sharī'ah principle which says: الأصل في الأشياء الإباح "The default in dealings is permissibility"

F) Generosity

Exchanging gifts and invitations with non-Muslims is part of the Prophetic tradition. Al-Ṭabarāni reported that the Prophet صلى الله عليه وسلم accepted a gift from al-Muqawqis, the chief of the Copts, and 'Umar RA sent a gift to his non-Muslim brother, as mentioned in Bukhāri. The Prophet صلى الله عليه وسلم was invited by a Jew to a meal of barley bread and rancid oil, and he accepted the invitation.

Caution: The same thing can be said for sincere strugglers amongst homosexual and transgender community members. One thing we should keep in mind during all this generosity is that it should not be

---

[123] Abu al-'Abbâs Aḥmad ibn Idrees al-Qarâfi. Al-Dhakheerah (Beirut: Dâr alGharb al-Islâmi, 1994), 10:240

[124] Muhammad ibn 'Ali ibn Daqeeq al-'Eed. Iḥkâm al-Aḥkâm (Cairo: Maṭba'at al-Sunnah al-Muḥammadiyyah, n.d.), 2:225.

[125] Aḥmad Ibn Ḥamdân, Al-ri'âyah al-ṣughrâ, 2:1276.

glorified in such a way that it serves as a desensitization for our kids, or a sense of approval.

G) Gentleness

Gentleness in speech and conduct is an Islāmic etiquette to be upheld with all people. Allāh says:

وَإِذْ أَخَذْنَا مِيثَاقَ بَنِي إِسْرَائِيلَ لَا تَعْبُدُونَ إِلَّا اللَّهَ وَبِالْوَالِدَيْنِ إِحْسَانًا وَذِي الْقُرْبَىٰ وَالْيَتَامَىٰ وَالْمَسَاكِينِ وَقُولُوا لِلنَّاسِ حُسْنًا وَأَقِيمُوا الصَّلَاةَ وَآتُوا الزَّكَاةَ ثُمَّ تَوَلَّيْتُمْ إِلَّا قَلِيلًا مِّنكُمْ وَأَنتُم مُّعْرِضُونَ۝

> "And [recall] when We took the covenant from the Children of Israel [enjoining upon them]: Do not worship except Allāh; and do good to parents and to relatives, orphans, and the needy. And speak to people with good [words]."[126]

This gentleness and speaking good words to people goes beyond niceness. When Ibn Wahb, the student of Imam Mālik, was asked about backbiting against a Christian, he cited this verse to show its prohibition.[127] Note that in Islāmic discourse, gheebah (backbiting) means speaking ill of them, albeit truthfully, in their absence.

This gentleness was particularly emphasized when preaching. When Allāh sent Mūsa AS and Hārūn AS (Moses and Aaron) to Pharaoh, He told them,

فَقُولَا لَهُ قَوْلًا لَّيِّنًا لَّعَلَّهُ يَتَذَكَّرُ أَوْ يَخْشَىٰ۝

> "And speak to him with gentle speech, so that perhaps he may be reminded or fear [Allāh]." [Ṭāhā 20:44]

---

[126] Surat al-Baqarah, Ayat 83

[127] 'Ali ibn Khalaf ibn Baṭṭâl. Sharḥ saḥiḥ al-Bukhâri (Riyadh: Maktabat al-Rushd, 2003), 9:247

We are told to be gentle even with those who are sly and offensive. It was reported that a group of Jews approached the Prophet صلى الله عليه وسلم and greeted him with twisted pronunciation, and said "as-sāmu 'alaykum, O Muḥammad!" (meaning, "may death and destruction come upon you") instead of as-salāmu 'alaykum. 'Ā`ishah RA heard them and responded by saying, "as-sāmu `alaykum" as well. The Prophet صلى الله عليه وسلم then said to 'Ā`ishah:

مهلا يا عائشة إن الله يحب الرفق في الأمر كله

"Easy, 'Ā`ishah; Allāh loves gentleness in all matters." She told him, "Did you not hear what they said?" He replied, "I did, and I responded by saying, 'And upon you.'"[128]

Caution: We shouldn't be naïve as a community, and this gentleness shouldn't give our own community and our Muslim youth the wrong message. Since we are a minority in the West, we need to have a balanced understanding of how to be gentle in our attitudes, and at the same time stand firm on our own principles regarding sexuality.

H) Social bonds with colleagues

Allāh says

وَاعْبُدُوا اللَّهَ وَلَا تُشْرِكُوا بِهِ شَيْئًا ۖ وَبِالْوَالِدَيْنِ إِحْسَانًا وَبِذِي الْقُرْبَىٰ وَالْيَتَامَىٰ وَالْمَسَاكِينِ وَالْجَارِ ذِي الْقُرْبَىٰ وَالْجَارِ الْجُنُبِ وَالصَّاحِبِ بِالْجَنبِ وَابْنِ السَّبِيلِ وَمَا مَلَكَتْ أَيْمَانُكُمْ ۗ إِنَّ اللَّهَ لَا يُحِبُّ مَن كَانَ مُخْتَالًا فَخُورًا

"Worship Allāh and associate nothing with Him, and to parents do good, and to relatives, orphans, the needy, the near neighbor, the neighbor farther away, the companion at your side, the traveler, and

[128] Agreed upon

those whom your right hands possess. Indeed, Allāh does not like those who are self-deluding and boastful." [129]

Ibn al-Qayyim explained, "The rights of everyone mentioned in this verse are binding, even if they were unbelievers."[130]

If social bonds with non-Muslims are not forbidden, then we can safely say that social bonds with sincere strugglers amongst homosexuals and transgenders will be fine as well. They may arise for reasons such as kinship or marriage, reasons of common interest, such as partnership or trade, or other reasons and commonalities, such as being neighbors, of the same profession, or compatriots. Man is predisposed to love those who are kind to him, and he may even be unable to resist loving a well-mannered neighbor.

Neighborliness is shown to all people regardless of their religion. Al-Qurṭubi commented in his tafsīr: "I say: based on that, kind treatment of neighbors is enjoined and is recommended, whether they are Muslim or not [...]. Kind treatment may be in the form of assistance, or it may be in the form of being kind, refraining from annoyance, and standing by them."[131]

Kindness toward one's colleagues and coworkers is a branch of neighborliness. It is about being good to people with whom you share the same space.

I) Sincere Concern for their future

Our natural love and friendship are extended by default to the human family, and confirmed for those who are kind to us (so any non-

---

[129] Surat al-Nisâ', Ayat 36

[130] Ibn Qayyim al-Jawziyyah, Aḥkâm ahl al-dhimmah (1997), 2:793.

[131] al-Qurṭubi, Al-jâmi' li aḥkâm al-Qur'ân, 5:183.

aggressive, sincere person struggling with homosexuality or transgenderism will be included in this).

We especially need to be concerned for their future if we see them struggling. Allāh reminds us over and over again of our common origin and brotherhood:

إِذْ قَالَ لَهُمْ أَخُوهُمْ لُوطٌ أَلَا تَتَّقُونَ

"When their brother Lūṭ said to them, "Will you not fear Allāh?" [al-Shu'arā` 26:161)

In these verses, Allāh mentions their brotherhood despite the fact that Lūṭ (AS) was preaching to his own tribe. This is clearly the brotherhood of humanity. One may also understand that Lūṭ AS was called "their brother", because after migrating to their land he became one of them. If Allāh can call Lūṭ AS a brother in humanity for the homosexual people, then we need to have a balanced approach when refuting them and deconstructing their worldview. Our concern should always be about goodwill and seeking eternal success for them, through the means of repentance, because the default is our shared membership with the human family. We should also act on behalf of humankind and plead with Allāh to save humanity.

For instance, Ibrāhīm AS also manifested this sentiment regarding the homosexual nation; Allāh says:

فَلَمَّا ذَهَبَ عَنْ إِبْرَاهِيمَ الرَّوْعُ وَجَاءَتْهُ الْبُشْرَىٰ يُجَادِلُنَا فِي قَوْمِ لُوطٍ

"And when the fright had left Abraham and the good tidings had reached him, he began to argue with Us concerning the people of Lūṭ." [Hūd 11:74]

Although "arguing" here means either pleading with Allāh to spare the people of Lūṭ, or the Muslims amongst them,[132] Ibrāhīm AS is clearly pleading to defer the punishment for the people of Lūṭ. Allāh explains that Ibrāhīm AS did that because it was part of his character:

إِنَّ إِبْرَاهِيمَ لَحَلِيمٌ أَوَّاهٌ مُّنِيبٌ ۝

يَا إِبْرَاهِيمُ أَعْرِضْ عَنْ هَـٰذَا ۝

"Indeed, Ibrāhīm was forbearing, grieving [i.e., hurt by human suffering] and [frequently] returning [to Allāh]." [Hūd 11:75} "O Ibrāhīm, give up this [plea]." [Hūd 11:76]

It was not to condemn his forbearance and grief for human suffering or his affection for his fellow humans, but the reason was explicitly stated to be:

إِنَّهُ قَدْ جَاءَ أَمْرُ رَبِّكَ ۖ وَإِنَّهُمْ آتِيهِمْ عَذَابٌ غَيْرُ مَرْدُودٍ ۝

"Indeed, the command of your Lord has come, and indeed, there will reach them a punishment that cannot be repelled."[133]

Final Caution

Being kind and courteous when dealing with the non-aggressive sincere strugglers, or adherents of other faiths, is an injunction of our religion.

---

[132] See the following tafsir:
a) Ibn Ashur, At-Tehrir Wa-Tanweer, 11\299.
b) Musaid bin Suleman At-Tayyar, Mawsooa' Tafsir Bil-Masur, 11\356, narration no. 35957, reported from Mohammad bin Ishaq.
c) Imam Islahi, Tadaur Quran, 4\157
d) Imam Alusi, Rooh-ul-Maani', 7/141-142
e) Imam Ar-Raazi, Tafsir-Al-Kabir, 18\376

[133] Surah Hūd, āyah 76

But treating them with kindness and justice does not require that we approve of their faith or their way of life. This is extremely important because Muslim minorities in the West already have a defeatist mentality, which is oftentimes reflected in non-Sharī'ah compliant interfaith activities in different Islāmic centers, and this can easily become a source of desensitization for the Muslim community, especially our youth.

Dealing with aggressive/influential individuals amongst homosexuals and transgenders

As we mentioned above, Muslims may certainly take a non-hostile sincere struggling Muslim or non-Muslim as a friend, have goodwill for them, and seek guidance for them, since we love guidance for ourselves. Also, the default concerning our relationships with the children of our parents, Ādam and Ḥawā`, is one of love and friendship.[134] Such a default is further confirmed for those who are fair, virtuous, and kind. As for those who viciously oppose Allāh and His Meṣsenger صلى الله عليه وسلم, and try to sway us from our religion, we extend to them, justice, not affection, and we won't give them any chance or opportunity to influence our youth or community. Yet, we still wish for their guidance, because we care for our entire human family. But our relationship with them will be very conservative, careful, and cautious.

---

[134] There are numerous reports about it, few of them are below:

A) We know Prophet's love for his non-Muslim uncle Abu Talib
B) we are supposed to love our non-Muslim wife if she is from the people of the book
C) Ibn Mas'ood who had a Christian companion and would greet him with salâm, and when asked about this, he replied, "It is the right of companionship (al-Qurṭubi, Al-jâmi' li aḥkâm al-Qur'ân, 11:112)

Final Caution regarding violence

The religion of Islām is a religion of mercy, and does not preach indiscriminate hatred, much less violence, against people on account of their feelings or urges.

It is a mistake to conflate teaching one's faith communities about moral and immoral acts with preaching hatred against people. As an example, Muslims believe that it is immoral to drink alcohol, yet it cannot be claimed that they preach violence against those who drink. Disapproving a particular act, or religiously disliking the lifestyle, does not translate into sanctioning acts of violence against an individual who practices those acts.

Furthermore, we welcome anyone intent on living an Islāmic lifestyle to our mosques and communities, regardless of their personal temptations or desires. We encourage all Muslims to provide others with any spiritual help and support they need, and to accommodate all people of all backgrounds as reasonably as possible and within the parameters of Islāmic law.

Regarding people outside the faith who adopt such practices, Islām does not ask us to mistreat anyone, and we advise Muslims to demonstrate to all people the kindness, compassion, and good manners emblematic of our faith as mentioned above, regardless of their personal practices. And if asked, or if the opportunity arises, we should present our beliefs with kindness and wisdom. While it is not obligatory to preach at every instance to every individual, if and when we are asked about Islām's doctrines and morals, we must be truthful and present them as they are, without compromising, hiding, or adjusting any principles.

Given the sensitive nature of these topics, and the ease with which misunderstandings can occur, we state explicitly that as citizens of the

United States of America, we recognize the diversity afforded by the political laws of this land, even as we insist on our own political and religious rights to preach our faith in its full integrity to all who decide to follow it.[135]

This entire discussion should lead us to our next subchapter: what does Islām say about passing moral judgment?

Revisiting the doctrine of "moral policing" or "don't judge me"[136]

Before we can understand the issue of moral judgment, let's understand the two extremes in our global community, and then we can discuss the issue at hand.

On one extreme, it is an undeniable fact that many of us Muslims are sickened by the inflamed polemics between Muslim preachers and activists, a problem that has become compounded by the here-to-stay phenomenon of social media. We must remember though, this is not limited to Muslims, or even to religious people in general. Any survey of social media will prove that. The number of refutation videos, posts, and tweets that are produced and targeted within our Muslim community, despite our common ground, has left significant confusion among the greater Muslim community.

However, this antipathy to poorly propounded polemics may push us towards the opposite extreme, that for decades has been promoted by many intellectual elites, and has become the ethos of certain cultural spaces, most notably, academia: to completely refrain from passing judgment. This is an idea based on the contemporary concept of moral

135 https://muslimmatters.org/2022/06/21/fatwa-regarding-transgenderism/

136 This Subchapter is taken from Dr.Hatem El-Haj's book: "Love and Hate in Islām", pages 27-48, with his permission and I am just summarizing it.

relativism, which has been energized by the prevalent postmodernist philosophy.

Moral relativism is on the other extreme

Moral relativism is the idea that there is no universal or absolute set of moral principles. It's a version of morality that advocates "to each their own", and those who follow it say: "Who am I to judge?"[137]

When we talk about moral relativism or postmodernism,[138] we must remind ourselves to stay fair and not be unthoughtful and reactionary. This philosophical school does have a negative reputation among religious people for obvious reasons. However, it is also to be remembered that there is usually a reason why a particular intellectual argument or trend may gain popularity and widespread acceptance. The main protagonists of moral relativism may have been influenced by the destruction of the "enlightened" man brought onto the world in the 19th and the first half of the 20th centuries, which culminated in World War II. Their moral relativism and deconstructionism may have been a scream in the face of human ignorance, arrogance, and conceit. Of course, we recognize how far it has gone, and how radical it has become. Yet, we must not rush to wholly oppose it without understanding its motives and goals.

An entire book could be written on the subject of passing moral judgment, so a comprehensive treatment is beyond the scope of this discussion. However, it is still related to the subject of etiquettes of

---

[137] Ethics unwrapped – McCombs School of Business – The University of Texas at Austin (https://ethicsunwrapped.utexas.edu/glossary/moral-relativism)

[138] Does Postmodernism mean Moral-Relativism because both considers the truth or reality to be subjective. Postmodern thought did not create this situation of moral relativism for sure, but it tries to explore its structures and it teaches the same moral and ethical relativism. Its comprehensive treatment is beyond the scope of this book. For more info, See: https://www.britannica.com/topic/postmodernism-philosophy/Postmodernism-and-relativism

dealing with or judging your sinful friend. Therefore, I will try in the following pages to find the golden mean, as I address the importance of passing moral judgment, and the Islāmic etiquette to guard against excess in this regard, so as to mitigate the untoward side effects, which could be catastrophic.

Is moral judgment avoidable?

It might be surprising, but we all have our own moral standards, and there is no way to avoid moral judgment. The notion of avoidance being the "right" thing, is in itself a moral judgment. There is no way to function in life without passing judgment in general, moral judgment in particular, and we do this all the time. We need it to protect ourselves from evil. We look for reviews of products and services to guide our purchase decisions. That is judging. We warn about pedophiles and other types of criminals. That is a moral judgment. We are repulsed by incest and indecent exposure. If a woman hears that a man frequents a brothel, she will likely be reluctant to marry him. Judges and jurors pass judgment all the time. If those laws being enforced are not based on any moral foundation, then they are simply a manifestation of tyranny, whether majoritarian or otherwise.

Even scientific data indicates that judgement is unavoidable, interested readers can look at this research in the footnotes.[139]

---

[139] Jean Piaget, The Moral Judgment of the Child, trans. Marjorie Gabain, 5th impr. (London: Routledge & Kegan Paul, 1968), 103.
Piaget, Moral Judgment of the Child, 2.
Joshua Greene and Jonathan Haidt, "How (and Where) Does Moral Judgment Work?," Trends in Cognitive Sciences 6, no. 12 (2002): 517, https://doi.org/10.1016/ s1364-6613(02)02011-9.
Mordecai Nisan and Lawrence Kohlberg, "Universality and Variation in Moral Judgment: A Longitudinal and Cross-Sectional Study in Turkey," Child Development 53, no. 4 (1982): 865, https://doi.org/10.2307/1129123, 865.
Greene and Haidt, "How (and Where) Does Moral Judgment Work?," 517

What is evil within the Islāmic paradigm?

As we discussed earlier on the subject of consequences of modernity and postmodernity, while humanity will forever be in need of the Ever-Living God, our consciousness of Him seems to have greatly suffered as a consequence of our conceit and childish excitement about our scientific achievements and Newtonian explanations of "natural" phenomena. Whatever Nietzsche meant by his ugly statement, "God is dead",[140] the reality of our world today is that humans have largely removed Him from the center of their thought, and the human worldview is no longer theocentric, but anthropocentric, or let us be honest and say, egocentric. Because of that, intellectuals have been trying to find another anchorage for morality away from the Divine Lawgiver. Whether it is categorical or utilitarian, neither invokes Him. But if you remove God and the Hereafter from the equation, as Elizabeth Anscombe cleverly pointed out, any "oughtness" ethics become incoherent.[141] As Allāh explains this concept:

ومن لم يجعل الله له نورا فما له من نور

" And he to whom Allāh has not granted light - for him there is no light."[142]

If we deny the divine guidance for morality, and if pain and pleasure, as we are told by utilitarian ethics, are the only basis for morality, we have still not solved the problem. How do we practically and accurately balance between intensity and extent, or intensity and probability? How do you ensure you are not being blindsided or short-sighted? Hasn't this so often been the case for human beings? What are the long-term

---

[140] Nietzsche, The Gay Science, 167

[141] Barbara Herman, "The Practice of Moral Judgment," The Journal of Philosophy 82, no. 8 (1985): 414-436, https://doi.org/10.2307/2026397, 414-415.

[142] Surah An-Noor, Āyah 40

consequences of extramarital relations? Has any community, past or present, been able to tame the beast of alcohol and mitigate its harms? What dollar value will you put on one human life in your calculations of competing interests? More importantly, what would make someone favor the greatest good for the greatest number over their own personal good?

I know the allergy some people have, especially in the West, to religion or divine guidance, but data have consistently shown the superior moral edge of people of faith. Psychologist Jonathan Haidt, an atheist himself, remarks: "Religious believers in the United States and in Europe are happier, healthier, longer lived, and more generous to charity and to each other than are secular people."[143]

In Islām, morality combines the deontological and teleological components with virtue ethics, but all of this is rooted in Divine grace and authority, and in human accountability before the All-Good God which God-Phobic philosophers can't comprehend.

The Sharī'ah also ranked for us the degrees of good and evil, to allow us to resolve conflicts of competing interests, although human wisdom will always be needed in order to do that successfully. While there is no substitute for human intellect, but it should be bounded and navigated properly within divine guidance.

In Islām, evil is not only that which causes immediate or easily foreseen pain. There are many evils whose harm may not be seen in the short term. Additionally, the rights of God are not trivialized, and their

---

[143] See Michael D. Magee, "Jonathan Haidt and the New Atheists: Moral Psychology and the Misunderstanding of Religion," Academia.edu, July 5, 2015, https://www.academia.edu/13658137/Jonathan_Haidt_and_the_New_Atheists_Moral_Psychology_and_the_Misunderstanding_of_Religion, 16.

violation is the greatest evil, and a precursor for all other evils. The Prophet صلى الله عليه وسلم said:

أَكْبَرُ الكَبَائِرِ: الإِشْرَاكُ بِاللَّهِ، وَقَتْلُ النَّفْسِ، وَعُقُوقُ الوَالِدَيْنِ، وَقَوْلُ الزُّورِ،

"The biggest of al-kabā`ir (the great sins) are to join others as partners in worship with Allāh, to murder a human being, to be undutiful to one's parents, and to make a false statement [or to bear false witness][144]

Notice the seamless harmony between the moral evils. The kind attitude we are commanded to exhibit toward people of other faiths never means that polytheism does not exist, or that we should not condemn it. Also, no amount of acrobatic hermeneutics can remove the negative meanings of the word "zinā" (fornication or adultery), or explain these verses in any way other than the obvious:

وَلُوطًا إِذْ قَالَ لِقَوْمِهِ أَتَأْتُونَ الْفَاحِشَةَ مَا سَبَقَكُم بِهَا مِنْ أَحَدٍ مِّنَ الْعَالَمِينَ

"And [We had sent] Lūṭ when he said to his people, "Do you commit such immorality as no one has preceded you with from among the worlds? Indeed, you approach men with desire, instead of women. Rather, you are a transgressing people." [Surat Al-'A`rāf 7:80]

Your good treatment of your coworker who happened to be involved in these sins or others, should never mean your acceptance of their wrong actions, nor should that be a requirement of civility. If I am confident that God declared something a sin, then it is, whether or not I comprehend all of its negative consequences on the person or society. Thankfully, all His non-ritual ordainments are comprehensible.

---

[144] Agreed upon

Limitations & Prerequisites of Islāmic Moral Judgement

It is important to understand before we talk about the etiquettes of judgment, the limitations of our judgment, particularly when we judge human behavior. What we are judging is the action and the actor in so far as they embody this act. We do not know their full story. After all, the Prophet صلى الله عليه وسلم told us of a worshiper who went to hell for locking up a cat and starving it to death, and of a prostitute who was forgiven for all her sins because she gave water to a thirsty dog. The ultimate judgment belongs to God alone. There are two major limitations in our judgments that we must be thoroughly aware of.

A) The first is that we judge the exterior behavior only.

B) The second is that our judgment is extremely temporal. We are unable to speculate, not only about our and others' final abode, but about our state and theirs at the end of the day.

There are numerous pieces of evidence for that, but a few of them are as follows:

1) Imām al-Ṭaḥāwi says, in his widely accepted creed:

"We do not declare any of them to be in Paradise or Hellfire. We do not allege their unbelief, idolatry, or hypocrisy, as long as they have not openly demonstrated anything of that. We leave their inner realities to Allāh Almighty."[145]

---

[145] Aḥmad ibn Muḥammad al-Ṭaḥâwi, Matn al-Ṭaḥâwiyyah, ed. Muhammad ibn Nâṣir al-Albâni (Beirut: al-Maktab al-Islāmi, 1414 AH), 67

2) Imām Ibn Ḥajar reported the consensus of the scholars: that judgment in this life is based on the exterior, and to Allāh alone belongs knowledge of the interior.[146]

3) In the following report the Prophet صلى الله عليه وسلم taught his beloved companion Usāmah ibn Zayd the gravity of judging the interior of people. When Usāmah killed a man in battle after the man had said, "There is no God but Allāh," and told the Prophet صلى الله عليه وسلم of that, he صلى الله عليه وسلم asked, "Who will save you from 'There is no God but Allāh' on the Day of Judgment?" Usāmah said, "O Messenger of Allāh, he uttered it out of fear of my weapon." The Prophet replied,

أَفَلَا شَقَقْتَ عَنْ قَلْبِهِ حَتَّى تَعْلَمَ أَقَالَهَا أَمْ لَا؟

"Did you tear his heart apart so that you learned whether he actually uttered it for this or not?[147]

Among the worst usurpations of Allāh's prerogatives is to adjudicate on His behalf without permission, thereby condemning people eternally. Jundub reported that Allāh's Messenger صلى الله عليه وسلم said:

أَنَّ رَجُلًا قَالَ: وَاللهِ لَا يَغْفِرُ اللهُ لِفُلَانٍ، وَإِنَّ اللهَ تَعَالَى قَالَ: مَنْ ذَا الَّذِي يَتَأَلَّى عَلَيَّ أَنْ لَا أَغْفِرَ لِفُلَانٍ، فَإِنِّي قَدْ غَفَرْتُ لِفُلَانٍ، وَأَحْبَطْتُ عَمَلَكَ

"A person once said [to another], 'Allāh would not forgive such and such (person).' Thereupon Allāh the Exalted and Glorious, said [to him]: 'Who is he who adjures about Me that I would not grant pardon to so-

---

[146] Aḥmad ibn Ḥajar al-'Asqalâni. Fatḥ al-Bâri fi Sharḥ Ṣaḥeeḥ al-Bukhâri (Beirut: Dâr al-Ma'rifah, 1959), 12:273.

[147] Sahih Muslim

and-so; I have granted pardon to so-and-so and blotted out your deeds"[148]

'Umar RA reminds us of the limitations of our judgment, and at the same time of the necessity and legitimacy of passing judgment. He said:

"In the lifetime of the Messenger of Allāh صلى الله عليه وسلم, some people were called to account based on revelation. Now that revelation has discontinued, we shall judge you by your apparent acts. Whoever displays to us good, we shall grant him peace and security, and treat him as a near one. We have nothing to do with his interior. Allāh will call him to account for that. whosoever shows evil to us, we shall not grant him security, nor shall we believe him, even if he professed that his intention was good."[149]

Etiquettes of passing moral judgment

Passing judgment is a precarious activity. As we have seen before, it can lead to destruction and damnation. There are two foundational questions to be asked every time we embark on any action: why, and how? The place we are coming from, and the worldview we have, can greatly affect our attitude toward this serious matter. Before we can discuss "how" i.e. the etiquettes of passing moral judgment, the more important question of the two is the "why" question, so let us see the prerequisites of it.

Prerequisites of passing moral judgment

A few things must qualify before we pass any moral judgment

---

[148] Sahih Muslim

[149] al-Bukhâri, from 'Abdullâh ibn 'Utbah ibn Mas'ood.

a) **Intention:** Our actions must all be sincere and devoted to God alone. When we pass judgment, avoid people, warn about them, or forbid them from evil, we must do that, when warranted, out of devotion to Allāh and compliance with His command. For verily, deeds are by their intentions, and verily, Allāh accepts none except those that are sincere and through which His pleasure was sought.

b) **Having Mercy:** Judging people morally or calling them out on their evil does not mean that you do not care for your fellow human beings.

An amazing part of the Qur`ānic story of the people Lūṭ (A.S.) regarding Ibrāhīm AS says:

فَلَمَّا ذَهَبَ عَنْ إِبْرَاهِيمَ الرَّوْعُ وَجَاءَتْهُ الْبُشْرَىٰ يُجَادِلُنَا فِي قَوْمِ لُوطٍ

"And when the fright had left Ibrāhīm and the good tidings had reached him, he began to argue with Us concerning the people of Lūṭ." [Hūd 11:74]

Although arguing here means pleading with Allāh either to spare the people of Lūṭ or the Muslims among them[150], Ibrāhīm AS still presented a counterargument. What is surprising, is how Allāh describes the character of Ibrāhīm that motivated this counterargument:

---

[150] See the following tafsir:

f) Ibn Ashur, At-Tehrir Wa-Tanweer, 11\299.

g) Musaid bin Suleman At-Tayyar, Mawsooa' Tafsir Bil-Masur, 11\356, narration no. 35957, reported from Mohammad bin Ishaq.

h) Imam Islahi, Tadaur Quran, 4\157

i) Imam Alusi, Rooh-ul-Maani', 7/141-142

j) Imam Ar-Raazi, Tafsir Al-Kabeer, 18/376

إِنَّ إِبْرَاهِيمَ لَحَلِيمٌ أَوَّاهٌ مُّنِيبٌ

"Indeed, Ibrāhīm was forbearing, grieving [i.e., hurt by human suffering] and [frequently] returning [to Allāh]."[151]

Ibrāhīm AS was advocating on behalf of his fellow man and pleading to God to spare them. That is not unexpected. Prophet Muḥammad صلى الله عليه وسلم, said:

خابَ عبدٌ وخَسِرَ لَم يجعلْ اللهَ تعالى في قلبهِ رحمةً للبشَر

"Man is doomed and a loser if Allāh does not put compassion for humankind in his heart"[152]

c) **Observing yourself:** Having a devotion to Allāh and mercy for people are two important prerequisites. The third one we must observe and keep in mind as well is "you." When we must pass judgment, we are doing that from the place of fellow sinners—those who are primarily worried about their survival, anxious about their sins, and fearful for themselves—not lords.

Abu Hurayrah RA narrated that the Messenger of Allāh صلى الله عليه وسلم said:

يُبْصِرُ أَحَدُكُمُ الْقَذَاةَ فِي عَيْنِ أَخِيهِ، وَيَنْسَى الْجِذْعَ فِي عينه"[153]

"One of you sees the mote in his brother's eye while forgetting the stump in his own eye"

---

[151] Surat Hood, Ayat 11:75

[152] Reported by al-Dulâbi in al-Kunâ wal-asmâ'; al-Albâni said in al-Silsilah alṣaḥeeḥah (456), "its chain is sound."

[153] Sahih Ibn Hibban

After we have learned about the place we must come from, we should now address the etiquettes of passing judgment. We can classify them into three phases: before, during, and after we pass judgment.

1) Before Passing Judgment

Before we pass judgment, we must first ensure that we should:

a) Not seek the mistakes of others

At times, we need to judge evil and falsehood as such. However, we are told by the Prophet صلى الله عليه وسلم that we should not be looking for people's shortcomings in order to expose them. Such is a malevolent attitude. The Prophet صلى الله عليه وسلم said:

يَا مَعْشَرَ مَنْ أَسْلَمَ بِلِسَانِهِ وَلَمْ يُفْضِ الإِيمَانُ إِلَى قَلْبِهِ، لاَ تُؤْذُوا الْمُسْلِمِينَ وَلاَ تُعَيِّرُوهُمْ وَلاَ تَتَّبِعُوا عَوْرَاتِهِمْ، فَإِنَّهُ مَنْ تَتَبَّعَ عَوْرَةَ أَخِيهِ الْمُسْلِمِ تَتَبَّعَ اللَّهُ عَوْرَتَهُ، وَمَنْ تَتَبَّعَ اللَّهُ عَوْرَتَهُ يَفْضَحْهُ وَلَوْ فِي جَوْفِ رَحْلِهِ

"O you who accepted Islām with their tongue, while faith has not reached their heart! Do not harm the Muslims, nor revile them, nor seek their shortcomings. For indeed whoever tries to expose his Muslim brother's secrets, Allāh exposes his secrets wide open, even if he were in the depth of his own house."[154]

Caution: The only exception to this is if there is any large benefit, e.g. if the influential personality who is followed by the masses is spreading mixed messages, then it's okay to verify his views in order to prevent public/collective harm. This is similar to how a scholar of ḥadīth went

[154] Sunan Abu Dawood

through serious scrutiny when verifying ḥadīth narrators. But this is an exception, not the general rule.

b) Verify what is relayed to you and overlook when overlooking is wise

Misinformation is pervasive in our current era, particularly on social media, where we are often presented with false information about individuals.

Allāh says:

يَا أَيُّهَا الَّذِينَ آمَنُوا إِنْ جاءَكُمْ فاسِقٌ بِنَبَإٍ فَتَبَيَّنُوا أَنْ تُصِيبُوا قَوْماً بِجَهالَةٍ فَتُصْبِحُوا عَلى مَا فَعَلْتُمْ نادِمِينَ

"O you who have believed, if there comes to you a disobedient one with information, investigate, lest you harm a people out of ignorance and become, over what you have done, regretful." [155]

There are many traditions to warn against gossipers and back-biters. It is also essential to realize that accepting other people's accounts as true is not without its own perils. Those people may be mistaken, or even malevolent. Many times, we deem people to be above failures of intent and judgment, when we truly do not know them well.

It was reported that a man testified on behalf of another man's credibility before 'Umar RA. He ['Umar] asked, "Are you his immediate neighbor who knows his comings and goings?" He [the man giving testimony] replied, "No." He ['Umar] asked, "Have you accompanied him on a trip that reveals people's good qualities?" He replied, "No." He ['Umar] asked, "Have you done any business with him to discover his pious scrupulosity?" He replied, "No." Whereupon 'Umar RA said, "I

---

[155] Surat al-Ḥujurât, Ayat 6]

think you just saw him at the mosque mumbling the Qur`ān and nodding his head with [its recitation]." He replied, "Yes." 'Umar RA responded, "Leave, you do not know him."[156]

Also, when overlooking is wise, then we should overlook:

Abu Hurayrah RA narrated that the Messenger of Allāh صلى الله عليه وسلم said:

رَأَى عِيسَى ابْنُ مَرْيَمَ عَلَيْهِ السَّلَامُ رَجُلًا يَسْرِقُ، فَقَالَ لَهُ: أَسَرَقْتَ؟ قَالَ: لَا وَاللَّهِ الَّذِي لَا إِلَهَ إِلَّا هُوَ، قَالَ عِيسَى عَلَيْهِ السَّلَامُ: آمَنْتُ بِاللَّهِ، وَكَذَّبْتُ بَصَرِي

"Jesus, son of Mary, peace be upon him, saw a man stealing, and said to him: Are you stealing? He [the man] said: No, by Allāh besides Whom there is no other God! Jesus, peace be upon him, said: I believe in Allāh and I disbelieve my eyes."[157]

The point being made here is twofold. The first is that your own senses may deceive you. The second is that overlooking people's mistakes by complete erasure from our minds is superior when we are not meant (or justified) to act on our knowledge.

c) Have good thoughts, give the benefit of the doubt, and look for excuses

It was reported by Ibn Abi al-Dunya RA that 'Umar RA said, "Don't presume any malevolence in a statement by a Muslim, as long as you find any way to interpret it charitably."[158]

---

[156] Abu Ḥâmid Muhammad ibn Muhammad al-Ghazâli, Iḥyâ' 'Uloom al-Deen (Beirut: Dâr al-Ma'rifah, n.d.), 2:82-83. al-'Irâqi considered it authentic

[157] Sunan An-Nissai, Grade: Sahih by Albani

[158] Ibn Abi Dunya

After verifying what you saw or heard, look for ways to interpret it charitably. Let your heart stay pure and safe from resentment and contempt for your brothers and sisters.[159]

Caution: This doesn't mean that we should become naïve, especially when the other person/group is acting in an aggressive way and they have a clear agenda.

2) While One is Passing Judgment

Now, without seeking any shortcomings, you have become aware of a person's supposed transgression. You verified it. There is no doubt. There are no excuses. What comes next?

Your judgment must be based on justice, knowledge, and deliberateness.[160]

First is **justice**. Allāh says:

﴿ يَا أَيُّهَا الَّذِينَ آمَنُوا كُونُوا قَوَّامِينَ بِالْقِسْطِ شُهَدَاءَ لِلَّهِ وَلَوْ عَلَىٰ أَنفُسِكُمْ أَوِ الْوَالِدَيْنِ وَالْأَقْرَبِينَ ۚ إِن يَكُنْ غَنِيًّا أَوْ فَقِيرًا فَاللَّهُ أَوْلَىٰ بِهِمَا ۖ فَلَا تَتَّبِعُوا الْهَوَىٰ أَن تَعْدِلُوا ۚ وَإِن تَلْوُوا أَوْ تُعْرِضُوا فَإِنَّ اللَّهَ كَانَ بِمَا تَعْمَلُونَ خَبِيرًا

"O you who have believed, be persistently standing firm in justice, witnesses for Allāh, even if it be against yourselves or parents and relatives. Whether one is rich or poor, Allāh is more worthy of both. So do not follow [personal] inclination, lest you not be just. And if you distort [your testimony] or refuse [to give it], then indeed Allāh is ever, with what you do, Acquainted."[161]

---

[159] It was reported by Ibn Abi al-Dunyâ that Umar (P.) said, "Don't presume any malevolence in a statement by a Muslim, as long as you find any way to interpret: it charitably. Ibn-Abi Dunya

[160] 'adl, 'ilm, and ḥilm

[161] Surat al-Nisâ', Ayat 135]

You notice that the verse addresses two types of bias. The first one is recognized by most people: we may favor ourselves and those close to us, and we must avoid that. The other type of bias is less obvious. Allāh teaches us that we should say the truth whether it is in favor of the rich or the poor, the strong or the weak. We should not let our empathy for the poor and weak make us sway from the truth and from justice. And this goes against postmodern and Neo Marxist paradigms, which want to destroy hierarchies on the basis of their conflict-based approach between the rich and the poor, or other presumed notions.

Interestingly, both these biases will come out of your love. There is a third kind of bias mentioned in the identical āyah in Sūrah Al-Mā`ida, Allāh says:

يَا أَيُّهَا الَّذِينَ آمَنُوا كُونُوا قَوَّامِينَ لِلَّهِ شُهَدَاءَ بِالْقِسْطِ ۖ وَلَا يَجْرِمَنَّكُمْ شَنَآنُ قَوْمٍ عَلَىٰ أَلَّا تَعْدِلُوا ۚ اعْدِلُوا هُوَ أَقْرَبُ لِلتَّقْوَىٰ ۖ وَاتَّقُوا اللَّهَ ۚ إِنَّ اللَّهَ خَبِيرٌ بِمَا تَعْمَلُونَ

"O you who have believed, be persistently standing firm for Allāh, witnesses in justice, and do not let the hatred of a people prevent you from being just. Be just; that is nearer to righteousness."[162]

What is exhibited in this āyah is how hate for someone can force you to be unjust. Because it's the love of the individual/group, or hate of the individual/group, which takes you away from justice and truth. There are many personal and social biases that we must watch out for. We are taught by the Prophet صلى الله عليه وسلم the need to break away from the ossified ungodly social molds that shape our thinking. There are many accounts in the tradition to this effect.

As for **judging with knowledge**, Allāh says:

---

[162] Surah Al-Maida, Āyah 8

وَلَا تَقُولُوا لِمَا تَصِفُ أَلْسِنَتُكُمُ الْكَذِبَ هَٰذَا حَلَالٌ وَهَٰذَا حَرَامٌ لِّتَفْتَرُوا عَلَى اللَّهِ الْكَذِبَ ۚ إِنَّ الَّذِينَ يَفْتَرُونَ عَلَى اللَّهِ الْكَذِبَ لَا يُفْلِحُونَ

"And do not say about what your tongues assert of untruth, "This is lawful and this is unlawful," to invent falsehood about Allāh. Indeed, those who invent falsehood about Allāh will not succeed."[163]

There is much to be said about this point. Before we judge others, we must have clear and comprehensive knowledge of the matter at hand. There are certain things all Muslims who were raised in a Muslim environment must be aware of, but even this is subject to the change of times and conditions. However, it is fair to say that a Muslim knows by necessity that stealing, adultery, the consumption of pork, and mistreatment of parents are ḥarām (forbidden). And that there are five daily mandatory prayers, and that fasting during the month of Ramaḍān is required. The rulings of many religious teachings do not possess this same level of clarity. Those who have comprehensive knowledge about these rulings may advise others regarding them. As for the clear rulings, religious advice concerning them may be extended in the proper way, and at the proper time, by anyone, to anyone.

As for **ḥilm (deliberateness)**

I mean by it: thoughtfulness, wisdom, and introspection, which all could be communicated through this beautiful word "ḥilm". You need a great pause. You need to verify that your judgment is not simply effective or based on your biases and prejudices. Allāh says:

---

[163] Surah Al-Naḥl, Verse 116

أَرَأَيْتَ مَنِ اتَّخَذَ إِلَـٰهَهُ هَوَاهُ أَفَأَنتَ تَكُونُ عَلَيْهِ وَكِيلًا(43")

"Have you seen him who has taken his own feeling/prejudice to be his God? Will you then be a constant trustee over him?"[164]

The word that is translated into prejudice in this verse is hawā, which means bias, prejudice, desire, feeling, and/or passion.

Many people, or dare I say, most people, follow their prejudice most of the time, especially in this regard. I find the following statement attributed to the American psychologist, William James, very insightful and eloquent: "A great many people think they are thinking when they are merely rearranging their prejudices."[165]

Many things may corrupt our fiṭrah, and consequently our judgment. Imām Ibn Taymiyyah mentioned, in different areas of his writings, seven: hawā (feeling/bias/prejudice), ẓann (conjecture), shubhah (misgiving), gharaḍ (ulterior motive), 'ādah (habit), taqlīd (blind following), and mawrūth (inherited beliefs).[166] It is important that you stay vigilant and aware of these obstacles to the truth that exist within you. A great spiritual and intellectual labor or investment is needed to guard against them on a regular basis.

---

[164] [Surah Al-Furqân, Verse 43]

[165] Gordon Pennycook, Jonathan A. Fugelsang, and Derek J. Koehler, "Everyday Consequences of Analytic Thinking," Current Directions in Psychological Science 24, no. 6 (2015), 425. http://www.jstor.org/stable/44318881.

[166] Carl Sherif El-Tobgui, Reason, "Revelation & the Reconstitution of Rationality: Taqī al-Dīn Ibn Taymiyya''s (d. 728/1328) Dar' Ta'ārud al-'Aql wa-l-Naql or 'The refutation of the contradiction of reason and revelation'" (PhD Thesis, McGill University, 2013), 284.

3) After Passing Judgment

When you observe some sin or wrongdoing, and you are able to make a fair, informed judgment about it, you should observe the following etiquettes.

A) Let it not cause you arrogance, despair, or carelessness

The Prophet صلى الله عليه وسلم said:

إذ قَالَ الرَجُل هَلَكَ النَّاس فَهُوَ أَهْلَكَهم

"When a person says: 'People have been ruined,' he is the most ruined of them all"[167]

Of course, this is when he says it out of arrogance or despair, not out of pain and grief.

B) Conceal

If the sin is done in private or within a small group, there is usually no benefit in publicizing it. In fact, when sins are publicized frequently, it could lead to detrimental effects on the community, such as:

a) Becoming desensitized to the sin

b) Losing trust in the community

c) Losing hope in the prospect of righteousness or the tenability of high moral standards

---

[167] Sahih Muslim from Abu hurayrah

Nu'aym narrated that Mā'iz came to the Prophet صلى الله عليه وسلم and admitted four times in his presence to having committed adultery, so he صلى الله عليه وسلم ordered that Mā'iz be stoned to death, but said to Hazzāl (the man who had advised Mā'iz to tell the Prophet صلى الله عليه وسلم about his sin):

لو سَتَرتَهُ بِثَوْبِكَ كَانَ خَيرًا لَكَ

"If you had covered him with your garment, it would have been better for you"[168]

Concealment is a virtue, one that Allāh chose for Himself. The Prophet صلى الله عليه وسلم said:

إِنَّ اللَّهَ عَزَّ وَجَلَّ حَلِيمٌ حَيِيٌّ سِتِّيرٌ يُحِبُّ الْحَيَاءَ وَالسَّتْرَ فَإِذَا اغْتَسَلَ أَحَدُكُمْ فَلْيَسْتَتِرْ

"Allāh, the Mighty, and Sublime, is forbearing, modest and concealing, and He loves modesty and concealment"[169]

Related to concealment, approaching the individual privately should be the preferred way, as it is more conducive to acceptance. The exception to this is someone who commits an indiscretion publicly, and cannot be advised in private, or refuses the advice. The purpose of public reproach would then be to alert the public to the evil of that action.

C) Forgive

If the sin was committed against you, and you can forgive it, use the opportunity to forgive while you are still in pain. Conquer your

---

168 Sunan Abu Dawood

169 Sunan An-Nissai

lowest tendencies at that time, and show magnanimity and grace. Allāh says:

وَلَا يَأْتَلِ أُولُو الْفَضْلِ مِنْكُمْ وَالسَّعَةِ أَنْ يُؤْتُوا أُولِي الْقُرْبَى وَالْمَسَاكِينَ وَالْمُهَاجِرِينَ فِي سَبِيلِ اللَّهِ وَلْيَعْفُوا وَلْيَصْفَحُوا أَلَا تُحِبُّونَ أَنْ يَغْفِرَ اللَّهُ لَكُمْ وَاللَّهُ غَفُورٌ رَحِيمٌ

"And let not those of virtue among you and wealth swear not to give [aid] to their relatives and the needy and the emigrants for the cause of Allāh, and let them [instead] pardon and overlook. Would you not like Allāh should forgive you? And Allāh is Forgiving and Merciful." [Al-Noor 24:22]

The one ordered to forgive here is Abu Bakr. He was ordered to forgive the man who falsely accused his daughter of being unchaste, causing enormous pain to him and his entire family. However, forgiveness here did not simply mean refraining from punishing the man. It meant that Abu Bakr should not stop sustaining him.

D) Avoid confrontation as much as possible and naming the offenders

While the Messenger of Allāh صلى الله عليه وسلم did command and forbid people directly, he would usually say, "Why are some people doing this or saying that?" 'Ā`ishah said: When the Prophet صلى الله عليه وسلم was informed of anything regarding a certain man, he would not say: What is the matter with so-and-so that he says such-and-such? But he would say:

مَا بَالُ أَقْوَامٍ يَقُولُونَ كَذَا وكَذَا

"What is the matter with people that they say such-and-such"[170]

[170] Sunan Abu Dawood

E) Avoid mockery and obscenity

There is just no room for such things in religious advice. They are categorically forbidden, and they are also counterproductive. Mockery is a satanic quality, and obscenity is plainly forbidden.

Final Caution:

These strict guidelines and prerequisites of passing moral judgment are neither an encouragement of tyranny, nor an effort to make an individual pessimistic about giving advice to his/her peers. Rather, one still has to enjoin the good and forbid the evil, but one has to keep these things in mind. Remember, if good people will live a life of monasticism and pessimism, then only evil will prevail.

Revisiting the doctrine of social justice[171]

This is a sensitive issue; many ask this question: is it sinful for Muslim activists and institutions to openly support LGBTQI+ organizations and rallies, under the guise of intersectionality? This requires more detail.

When homosexuality is viewed as an identity instead of an action, the withholding of moral approval from homosexual acts and disapproval of the gay identity, come to be seen as a rejection not of a discrete set of sinful acts and a problematic self-conception, but of the very person themselves. It is precisely for this reason that people objecting to homosexual activism are seen not as individuals with a specific moral claim about what does and does not constitute acceptable sexual behavior, but as retrograde, hateful bigots. In such a setting, few feel confident in saying as little as, "of course homosexual acts are ḥarām."

---

[171] I am just presenting you the summary of Ustadh Mobeen Vaid's article on this issue. For more detail, Pls read: https://muslimmatters.org/2022/01/07/where-the-rainbow-ends-american-muslims-lgbt-activism/

Add to this the fear of political marginalization, on top of the defeatist mentality as a Muslim minority, and the moral imperative to stand for the truth has become increasingly challenging for Muslims in the West, with the rise of such an organized LGBTQI+ movement. We are often told that being critical of the LGBTQI+ movement is being "on the wrong side of history."

In the face of all this, many Muslim communities in America have demonstrated little willingness to resist these cultural forces, opting most often to stand behind the movement as a matter of public advocacy. This capitulation to LGBTQI+ promotion has been especially pronounced among Muslim civil rights organizations and "non-Sharī'ah compliant" social justice activists.

Interestingly, major scholars and influencers, who are still considered traditional by Western standards, played a significant role in this capitulation with their silence on certain issues, as well as repeated acts of political support for LGBTQI+ in the name of social justice. As a result, the "lay-Muslim" has become increasingly desensitized to supporting LGBTQI+ individuals and initiatives. Those scholars and activists see their actions as a lesser evil, compared to coming out with full refutation and deconstruction of homosexual and trans arguments. Their argument for why their actions were justified has always been from the point of view that both Muslims and LGBTQI+ are considered minorities. Therefore, some of them thought it would be politically unwise to further ostracize Muslims by having them rally against a "fellow minority". I love these scholars for the sake of Allāh, but the truth is more beloved to me than any individual. Their actions have indeed harmed us collectively, as support for the LGBTQI+ has become black and white, which is a bigger evil.

Their silence on this issue, compounded with their support for LGBTQI+ social justice, sends a message to our Muslim community that this is okay and normal.

I do not see how it is any different from Muslims openly supporting corporations of alcohol under the guise of capitalism, or casinos under the guise of free living. In fact, it is much worse, because beer companies are not having annual parades, they don't have flags to hoist up, they don't push for more media representation, they're not changing how our children are taught in elementary schools, or changing what our kids are watching on TV, etc.

For Muslims who are inclined towards such activism, they must read the following, as Ustadh Mobeen said:

> "The core elements of the homosexual and transgender movements are immoral, as they normalize, promote, and celebrate behaviors and actions that constitute patent transgressions of the Divine command. It is imperative that Muslims not lose sight of this elementary fact."

What are some of the rights that Muslims are being asked to support with the LGBTQI+ movement?

The term "LGBTQI+ rights" as used in this piece encompasses a wide range of claimed rights. Though some are already recognized in law, such as same-sex marriage, "LGBTQI+ rights" refers mainly to the many proposed measures that are still under deliberation. Such measures include efforts to change school curricula by introducing critiques of gender, masculinity, femininity, and "heteronormativity", while also changing sex-specific spaces, such as bathrooms and locker rooms into "gender-identifying" ones. The push for "gender-identifying" spaces seeks to supplant the notion of gender, as defined by sex, with the notion of gender identity as a self-chosen psychosocial reality, which then determines the facilities one uses, the sports one plays, and the way one must be spoken to. LGBTQI+ rights also refer to those measures that continue to impinge on religious communities. These include the Equality Act's explicit subordination of religious freedom, pushes for the integration of sexual orientation and gender identity ("SOGI") education into school curricula, without so much as an opt-out possibility, and deliberations over "affirmative therapy" as the only permissible intervention for gender dysphoria or dissatisfaction with one's homosexual thoughts and desires. Meanwhile, the term "LGBTQI+ advocacy" as used in this piece, refers to all that goes above and beyond the explicitly political. It denotes the unceasing public program of indoctrination, and the shoehorning of LGBTQI+ themes into all corners of life, including public libraries and the media, the rewriting of history, and the refracting of LGBTQI+ issues and perspectives into myriad disciplines and endeavors—including, pertinently, religion.

In light of the foregoing considerations, it is our contention that:

1. All the aforementioned LGBTQI+ rights and advocacy efforts are unequivocally harmful to society
2. Such rights and advocacy efforts can have no reasonable political or theological justification for Muslims
3. Those specifically restricting their support for LGBTQI+ to limited anti-discrimination protections have no need to advocate for them, as such protections have long since been passed into law. Therefore, continuing to appeal to them serves purpose other than the further curtailment of religious freedoms and conscientious objection

LGBTQI+ advocacy is not merely about accommodating a small community that identifies as gender or sexually atypical; rather, it actually serves to induce sexual and gender confusion, while promoting LGBTQI+ lifestyles as liberating and worthy of unending celebration. The fomenting of gender and sexual confusion is evidenced in the rising number of youth who identify as LGBTQI+, as well as the growing "sampling" of same-sex experiences. The proliferation of sexual immorality sullies the soul of a society, while unquestioned support for LGBTQI+ rights and advocacy produces spiritual crises, with religious teachings that run counter to the LGBTQI+ perspective reported as a major cause of apostasy across religious boundaries in recent years.

But what about the "cooperate in righteousness and piety" argument?

The āyah which is often quoted regarding working with non-Muslims in common good is as follows:

وَتَعَاوَنُوا عَلَى الْبِرِّ وَالتَّقْوَىٰ ۖ وَلَا تَعَاوَنُوا عَلَى الْإِثْمِ وَالْعُدْوَانِ

"And cooperate in righteousness and piety, but do not cooperate in sin and aggression." (Sūrah Al-Mā`ida, āyah 2)

Some also mention the incident of the Treaty of Virtue during the life of the Prophet صلى الله عليه وسلم, where he made a pact with non-Muslims in which they agreed not to support oppressors over the oppressed in Makkah.[172]

The misunderstanding which some people develop from this incident is if that the Sharī'ah permits shirk—overt idolatry—to exist within its political boundaries, anything less than shirk should enjoy similar accommodation. So on what grounds should Muslims feel compelled to

[172] Fatḥ al-Bārī 4/473

oppose LGBTQI+ rights? The reservations of Muslims who object to LGBTQI+ rights are therefore regarded as more of a cultural taboo, rather than something that could compromise their religious integrity. After all, if the Sharī'ah can permit the practice of idolatry—the most heinous sin in the eyes of Allāh—within the borders of Dār-ul-Islām, then surely it can allow Muslims in a non-Islāmic polity to tolerate sexual transgression, no?

Perhaps the most obvious and immediate retort to this argument is to ask whether Muslims should then have any moral concerns for society at all? If they can permit non-Muslims' shirk, rightly highlighted as an abominable crime against Allāh, then, through this reasoning, we would be right to ask why we cannot simply be pleased for them to permit everything? What rationale would there be for advocating any limits on the desires of non-Muslims? If our tolerance for the reprehensible begins with shirk, then why care about income inequality? Or the environment? Or violence against women? Why should Muslims care about criminal justice reform? Should we simply remain silent on debates over legalizing gambling, narcotics, prostitution, and more?

It goes without saying that just about any concern we have for the world around us—short of shirk, of course—will, by definition, fall below the line of open idolatry. The mere idea of Muslim politics would be practically eliminated under such a rubric. There are more arguments, of course: the fact that the Sharī'ah did not categorically accept shirk without stipulations and controls, or without instituting incentives to convert to Islām as part of its political program (the khilāfah was hardly a shirk free-for-all); the fact that the Sharī'ah prohibited much that falls within the domain of social morality, such as prostitution and public indecency; the fact that Allāh and His Messenger صلى الله عليه وسلم condemned the Quraysh's practice of infanticide when the Muslims had no political power to speak of, and were a beleaguered and weak minority; the sociological and cultural consequences and direct effect of

LGBTQI+ advocacy, and the passage of LGBTQI+ rights on Muslims generally, and the acute effects on young Muslims specifically; the practical irrelevance of Muslim "support" for causes like LGBTQI+, given the diminutive size of the community and its consequent lack of meaningful influence on high-stakes public debates; and more, though this will suffice for now.

So what's the point?

This is not a call for Muslims to become Republicans or Democrats. On LGBTQI+ rights, Republicans and Democrats are far more bipartisan in their support than public debate would lead one to believe, even if important differences exist regarding where the two parties fall in some current debates. What this is, however, is a call for Muslims to transcend partisan political interests, to move past thinking of every issue of political or social concern through the prism of which party serves us best (as imperfect as that service is in either case), and to become comfortable standing up for and speaking the truth, even at the expense of public ostracism. We need to remember that Allāh's Prophets ministered to people who often rejected them. The truth can be a bitter pill for those habituated to falsehood.

How numerous are the verses and Prophetic teachings that tell us to command the good and forbid the evil? Indeed, the very act of doing so is essential to a faithful adherence to Allāh's path. And this leads to our conclusion.

Conclusion:

Resorting to divine guidance is the only solution

As we are concluding this research, even in current conditions, the sociological winds do not appear to be in our favor. Recent polling shows that support for gay marriage in the United States stands at seventy percent.[173]

We need to be attentive to political realities, and it would be foolish to propose politics that do not at least acknowledge how many LGBTQI+ rights are beyond debate in the current socio-political climate. Nonetheless, there remains important ongoing deliberation as to how LGBTQI+ rights should be negotiated, for those who maintain moral reservations regarding homosexual acts and transgenderism. Though there is no telling where all these debates will land, it should be expected that many will be decided in ways that are prejudicial to the interests of religious communities like our own. Some issues will be adjudicated by the courts, while others will be subject to the deliberative mechanics of public opinion and majoritarian politics, which are fickle and subject to alteration over time.

There are also many reasons to be discouraged by what the future might hold for Western Muslims. Religions in the West before us have largely collapsed at the altar of homosexuality/inclusivity, and are quickly proving incapable of resisting transgenderism, too. Some non-scholarly Muslim figures, who have built public reputations through social justice work, have come out strongly in support of LGBTQI+ rights, while lesser-known personalities have similarly been unequivocal in their support of Pride Month. Having said that, we should keep in mind our limitations, as well as remind ourselves that it is Allāh who is in control of our affairs,

---

[173] https://news.gallup.com/poll/350486/record-high-support-same-sex-marriage.aspx

not us. I want my beloved reader to note that there is a light at the end of the tunnel, so long as we do not succumb to conformity, and that light is the light of divine guidance. As Muslims, we have the ability to reform society, or at least substantially influence the direction in which society is headed, so long as we are united in not watering down the religion to fit into the current secular paradigm. The only medicine to this disease is to resort back to the Islāmic paradigm of sexuality. I know some of my beloved readers might be skeptical about even considering an Islāmic solution to sexuality, because of either European precedent with Christian theocracy, or (incorrect) preconceived notions about Islām itself. Let me explain why Islām is the only solution, to not only this sexual chaos, but also for every issue with which the West is struggling with right now.

Some problems have been an issue for various societies for quite some time, but we have not been able to solve them as a collective due to the lack of reliance on divine guidance. Trying to parse through these issues without Allāh's help has left us swinging from one extreme to the other, like a pendulum that goes back and forth without any benefit. Listed below are a few such issues that have plagued the societal collective, which can be solved if we were to just fully accept Allāh's guidance on these matters.

1) **Social problems**

Society is fluid and dynamic; what was yesterday is no longer today. But for a society to endure, there have to be some persisting values that can inform a societal structure. These include very basic things like the rights of individual people: what are the rights of men versus women? Should they be identical? Are there differences in value based on skin color? Do rights change over time? Who gets to decide these rights? etc.

These types of questions seem almost silly to us because we live in a society where these questions were largely answered before our time, and yet, we see some of these questions coming back today. The Western society we live in is a postmodern society that has become godless. As a result, our society tried to create its own social science to answer the aforementioned questions, but ended up lost between newly constructed movements like feminism and masculinism, and so many other "isms". The reason for this aimlessness is simply that postmodern Western society has abandoned divine guidance, along with reason itself. Due to the rise in radical inclusivity and identity politics, and the ever-shifting rubric with which "right" is defined, even reason has come into question and can be considered speculative.

As Muslims, however, our belief is that Allāh is our creator, and as our creator, He can guide us to the correct way of living in society. It is He who created men and women to have different yet complementary roles to each other, and it is He who restricted our freedom in specific areas so that we can find true peace and contentment in our relations. It only makes sense that divine guidance is the best answer to our problems; who would know more about the intricacies of the interactions between men and women than the one who created them in the first place? This same reasoning applies to different aspects of society as well, including racial issues, family structure, civil matters, etc. For a society to truly enjoy justice and informed equality between its people, the only real solution is that of divine guidance.

2) Dichotomy of Sex and Spirituality

One might think that the spheres of sexuality and spirituality are completely removed from one another and share no overlap. But the truth is, our spirituality informs our sexuality, such that it returns back to spirituality. Let's see how.

When society removes divine guidance from sexuality, we end up with an "either or" situation. Either we put preference towards sex/bodily pleasure and dismiss spirituality whilst doing so (e.g., hedonism), or we nourish the soul and demonize sex/bodily pleasure to achieve greater spirituality (e.g. monasticism). This dichotomous view is harmful to the individual and to the collective and can lead to extremes in both directions. Rather, we believe that Allāh gives us divine guidelines on how to enjoy sex/bodily pleasure, whilst also not falling into an animalistic type of unabashed indulgence. Islām teaches us that by engaging in lawful sex (i.e. through marriage), we are actually engaging in an act of worship. But how can that be? The Prophet صلى الله عليه وسلم informed us that engaging in unlawful sex leads to sin, so then the reverse is also true: engaging in lawful sex results in a reward. This genius arrangement allows the Muslim to nourish their spirituality through their bodily desires, with the reverse being true as well; if a Muslim restricts themselves only to their spouse, they fulfill their desires through their effort to maintain their spirituality. This demonstrates that Islām is truly a "sex-positive" religion, and that any other form of sex-positivity is often just a sham to engage in more promiscuity.

3) Political problems

In every school, a child will eventually learn about the different types of governments in the world. They'll read about democracies, monarchies, authoritarian/totalitarian regimes, etc. Most of these political systems do not consider any divine guidance, particularly with regards to sexual expression. Their anti-theistic tendencies are the result of the aversion to religion society acquired after the Renaissance in Europe, which relegated god to a private figure, rather than one that informs public dealings. Aside from their inherent lack of spirituality, each one of these has its fair share of problems, but we will look at the most prevalent one among them. Living in the West, we are primarily exposed to a capitalist democracy, which is touted as the most advanced and progressive type of governance. However, we have seen an increasing amount of polarization within said system, with conservatives and liberals becoming mortal enemies rather than political parties. Clearly, this bipartisan setup is not the best solution. Most of these systems are operational today simply by virtue of the fact that they have been around for so long. But most are built on fundamentally flawed foundations and those flaws can surface even in the postmodern age. We are seeing increasing tensions over issues like gun control and abortion rights; things that these 'progressive' governments should have worked out by now. Because these forms of governance are based on limited human reasoning, they inevitably run into walls and have to create workarounds for their own lack of understanding (amendments). The Islāmic form of governance, however, is not a comprehensive manual on exactly how to run a government. Rather, Islām places injunctions as guard rails to reign in these large political powers. One might think that this means Islām is 'lacking' a proper governance plan; quite the opposite. Instead, Islām recognizes how multifaceted a nation can be, and anticipates a pluralistic society. So instead of having many specific laws, it has fewer, but more broad rules that society must stay within. These rules are based upon Islāmic theology, ideology, and agreed upon legislation. This allows a society to flourish according to its socio-geographical position, and allows for wildly varied societies to exist under one type of governance. This is because Islāmic governance forms an ideological state, where each region, no matter its cultural diversity, adheres to a singular ideology, led by a single figure (the Khalīfah). This brings uniformity, not just in socioeconomic or political matters, but moral issues and public matters as well. That is the difference between a theistic society (i.e., Muslim rule) and a theocracy (e.g. Dark Ages Europe).

4) Economical problems

Zooming in slightly, we go from governance to commerce, arguably a sphere of modern living of equal import and greater relevance. After removing God from public life, postmodern society realized it didn't need to abide by any of the archaic commerce rules it once bent to. As a result, postmodern societies feature many predatory monetary structures whose aims are to increase the wealth of those already in possession of wealth, and to take wealth from those already lacking wealth. When interest/usury is let loose on society, it creates oxymoronic situations like that of the country of Nigeria, which borrowed 5 billion dollars on interest. After some years, the President of Nigeria announced that the country had paid back 16 billion dollars, and still had 28 billion dollars left to pay back! While you may read this and think that this is just an exaggerated example, the truth is that this same type of arrangement is rampant in the housing market (or any interest-based loan agreement), but just at a smaller scale. The Islāmic model of finance is meant to prevent such ludicrous situations, and unlike with governance, it does provide specific rules for transactions and money handling. Following the Islāmic model rids a society of such predation, and allows for money to consistently flow from the rich to the poor, ensuring money does not concentrate unfairly in the hands of a few.

5) Ethical/Moral problems

In terms of ethics, there is a plethora of choices one can use to inform how they act: categorical ethics, deontological, duty-based, consequentialist, teleological, etc. Many "thinkers" of the past have used their own reasoning to come up with systems of ethics/morality to solve ethical conundrums and navigate moral quandaries. Individuals like Kant, Aristotle, Plato, Aquinas, etc., all of them ended up with differing views on ethics. So how is one to choose? Again, by employing just a little bit of common sense, we realize that the one best suited to inform our ethics/morals is the one who created us: Allāh. By following the Islāmic model of ethics/morals, we arrive at a solution that protects the honor and dignity of all, without encroaching on the rights of others unjustly, and gives each individual a sense of safety and protection.

The Problem with Viewing Islām Through a Postmodern Lens: Are We Forcing a Square Peg into a Round Hole?

You may be wondering why we are even discussing the implementation of Islām in our collective lives when we have witnessed the state of Muslim countries that have attempted to do the same. It may appear that the postmodern West is doing much better than those Muslim countries. However, I would like to point out that what you have observed in those Muslim countries is, in fact, a diluted version of Islām that has been molded and contorted to align with Western principles. On top of their distortion of Islām, most Muslim countries suffer from the effects of colonial imperialism, as well as being ravaged by non-Muslim militaries that have left them in ruins. Rather, what you need to do is learn the pure, unadulterated form of Islām, and see for yourself how it is truly the solution to all of our problems. A simple example to illustrate this point is one trying to force a square peg into a round hole. Can it be done? If it were forced, either the peg would lose its original shape or break in order to fit into the hole. This is something even a toddler understands, as the peg and the hole are fundamentally different. Likewise, attempting to shape Islām to conform to postmodern western philosophies, such as liberalism, can lead to the same outcome. There are fundamental differences between a liberal worldview and an Islāmic worldview. In Islām, the highest authority is God, and we abide by His divine law, changing our desires based on His guidance, and having a sense of accountability based on the Hereafter. How then, can Islām be compatible with the modern secular/liberal worldview, which is diametrically opposed to those beliefs?

Conversely, the Western world views Islām through a postmodern liberal lens, limiting it to a personal religion rather than a societal one. This is due to the fact that a multitude of personal belief systems can exist under a separate, single, umbrella societal system. As a result, most of the religions in the West have been reduced to nothing but personal belief systems, instituted by a single person whenever they feel like it. But only a societal religion can effectively regulate matters such as morality, social laws, criminal laws, etc. at the societal scale. Suppose we were to disassociate Islām from the social, economic, and political spheres, and reduce it to only individual acts. In that case, some of the teachings of Islām would appear irrelevant and incoherent, as these teachings need to be viewed from a collective perspective. This is how the West views Islām, if they are even viewing it earnestly to begin with. Thus, instead of seeing Islām as the solution, it is seen as the problem. Islām offers a comprehensive approach that provides guidance at all levels - individual, small groups, and society at large. For example, Islām restricts sexual relations to marriage and forbids pre-marital sexual relations. This restriction not only brings peace to individuals, but also remedies a number of societal maladies, and creates a society that is freed from issues that plague modern-day societies. Furthermore, Islām provides divine legislative punishments for those who do not adhere to its guidelines, to enforce ethics and values at a societal level. How can one then attempt to address things, like ḥijāb or gender interactions, in isolation from the bigger picture? Doing this leads to one seeing those guidelines as backward or outdated, because they would be attempting to take a sliver of Islām and applying it at scale in a postmodern liberal world that preaches personal autonomy and freedom above all else.

There are inconsistencies between what society values and the teachings of pure Islām. As a result, when we turn to pure Islām, we may struggle to appreciate its beauty objectively. For instance, a society conditioned to value nudity will not appreciate modesty, and may instead disparage it. Similarly, a society that highly regards the unrestricted exercise of personal choice will not value submission to God. Trying to modify Islām to fit into constantly changing societal norms can be an arduous task, since these norms are highly volatile and rapidly changing. Therefore, rather than changing Islām, we must strive to change societal conditioning, and restore our ability to recognize the true worth of Islāmic values.

In short, there is no solution to our social struggles until we realize the NEED of going back to divine guidance. This is why the first chapter of the Qur`ān (Al-Fātiḥah) is such an amazing sūrah, because it reminds Muslims in every prayer that we are in desperate need of Allāh's guidance in our collective affairs.

اهدنا الصراط المستقيم

"O Allāh guide us all collectively to the straight path"

We ask that Allāh to raise us among those who lived righteously in this world, that He frees us from His blame, and that He blesses our efforts such that others may take heed. Ameen.

And Allāh knows best.

Chapter 7: FAQ

1. What is the best way to answer the question: "What does Islām say about homosexuality?"

The term homosexuality is a term which is loaded with identity politics. When answering this question, it's important that we first establish the premise that is being assumed: I should be able to act on my feelings. So then what about the adulterer, thief, and murderer? If we follow the current rhetoric used to justify homosexuality, then the aforementioned groups cannot be blamed; they were born that way. If a homosexual individual can claim that they were made like this, and that they're only acting on their feelings, these other acts should be permissible as well. We can easily see how this is a false argument which ultimately invalidates not just divine law, but secular law as well.

We must distinguish between feelings/desires, acts, and identity (as they are all separate in Islām, not combined into one). There's a difference between having same-sex desires, performing homosexual acts, and considering yourself to have a separate identity because of those feelings/acts.

What the LGBTQI+ community isn't able to realize is that these three things: desires, actions, and identity, are all different and cannot be merged into one.

Thus, in Islām, homosexuality as a desire is forgiven, as long as it's not acted upon, and if a person is patient with those desires (meaning he does not act on them). If that is the case, then he will actually be rewarded for struggling against those desires.

Homosexuality, as an action, is considered a major sin by all scholars. In today's society, if a person gets involved in this action, then he should immediately repent and know that God is Ever-Forgiving.

Homosexuality, as an identity, is confusing. Your sexuality shouldn't be used as your identity. Just as we do not proudly claim to be liars or thieves, we shouldn't identify ourselves based on our worst actions.

This extends to questions about LGBTQI+, as they are often questions about identity, rather than divine law.

What are the implications of accepting the Western sexual identity framework?

Identity framework changes the discussion; it omits moral concerns, and frames the issue as one of social justice (defined subjectively), as opposed to God's command, which is paramount and itself embodies perfect justice.

Back in the 1980s, the acronym LGBTQI+ didn't exist, only the word homosexuality existed. People used to say, what do you think about homosexuality? It was understood that you are asking about specific actions, as well as your moral opinion about them. (FYI most people in the 1980s would have said it's wrong)

Nowadays, the question is not about action, the question is, as Muslims, do we support their identity, which turns the question into: where do we stand on LGBTQI+ rights?

So within just a few decades, the question went from "where do you stand on the morality of an action?" to "where do you stand on the civil rights of a discrete minority?", forgetting what the action might be at all. Boiling it down even further, the question is really asking:

"do you believe in equality, freedom, and justice? Or are you just a bigot who hates people?" That's the conversation today! This is the direct result of the identity paradigm.

2. **Will I be punished if I have same-sex attraction?**

The way to answer this is to ask yourself: is it desire, action, or identity?

If it's just a matter of feelings or desires, then remember that there are faithful Muslims who experience same-sex attractions and/or gender dysphoria, and it is possible that a person may be sexually attracted to members of their own sex, either exclusively or partially. In fact, our early classical Fiqh scholars also affirm the possibility of these same-sex feelings.[174]

You might compare yourself with the people of Lūṭ AS, but that is a false comparison. The people of Lūṭ AS *acted* on their desires, whereas and you only have the desires. Therefore, these are two different things, and if you can control the desires, you will get reward for doing so.

This is a very real problem, and every community has a small number of people with same-sex attraction. But we need to understand that this desire is just like the desire of heterosexual people. If I see an attractive woman and have a desire for her, I must exercise patience and not commit any act of fornication or adultery. Doing so results in reward. Similarly, if those with same-sex attraction are being patient and not following their desires, then they too will also be rewarded.

---

[174] Sharh Muslim (4/31), Majmoo' al-Fataawa (15/413) and (21/245)

However, if someone acted on their same-sex desires, then we will ask them to do tawbah, just like a person who may have committed an act of fornication or adultery.

But what if a person starts identifying themselves as gay or trans? Islām does not define or categorize people on the basis of internal feelings. It's important for us to know that we are not a separate identity simply based on our sexual feelings or desires. Even if we act on those desires, we are still Muslims like everyone else.

Muslims struggling faithfully with same-sex attraction or Gender Identity Disorder should be embraced and supported, as they are showing patience and respecting the laws of Allāh despite their desires. Also, we as a community must realize that those people struggling with their feelings cannot simply be turn their feelings on and off like a switch, it's much deeper than that. Those who are seriously struggling, should be appreciated for their struggle against their desires and not acting in a ḥarām way.

Having said that, we must avoid the pitfalls of the gay identity paradigm. It completely destroys the moral discourse of Islāmic law because doing so will make the rulings of the Sharī'ah on homosexuality look outdated, as the issue will be one of identity rather than actions. Also, this is a trap for individuals. Accepting the identity paradigm can lead one to think things like: "maybe I was born as a man in a woman's body... maybe this is who I really am." Don't identify yourself based on your sexual desires or sexual orientation; that doesn't define who you are at your core. This act of identifying one's entire being on who they desire to sleep with is unprecedented in the history of humanity.

This idea of identifying based on your desires is a social construct of the postmodern West. It is neither universal nor Islāmic, neither is it endorsed by revelation nor reason. This is because, as we discussed multiple times, postmodernity doesn't consider either one, and it gives supreme authority instead to the feelings.

At the same time, if someone comes to you, who has identified as gay for the last 20 years, you can't expect that if you tell them to just not identify as gay that they will suddenly understand the fallacy of the identity paradigm. These things take time, so give them resources, talk to them, mentor them without compromising on your principles, and remember to be patient while they heal. It will take time to undo the effect of being raised in a western society inundated by identity politics.

3. **Can someone with same-sex attractions ever hope to marry the opposite gender and have a family after they repent from their same-sex lifestyle?**

In my humble opinion, one of the mistakes we make as Muslims is to think that there is no remedy for this disease, and that the homosexual can never become straight. If that were the case, then Allāh would not have told the people of Lūṭ AS to repent, and Lūṭ AS himself would not have called them to give up their perversion. Allāh is the Creator of man, and He knows what can be changed and what cannot. So do not pay any attention to any claim that is contrary to that (especially a therapist that bases their understanding in Freudian psychology).

How many individuals struggling with same-sex desires have turned to their Lord and repented, and their repentance has been accepted, and they have changed their ways, and their same-sex desires have disappeared? Lūṭ AS called on his people to marry, because that is an effective remedy in which the one who is affected by this ailment can direct his desires in a permissible manner. Are we smarter than

Prophet Lūṭ AS who suggested marriage as a remedy to same-sex attraction? [175]

4. **What do we need to do as a community if we are to deal with these issues effectively?**

We need to thoroughly understand the Islāmic gender and sexuality paradigm, and strongly stand in the face of differing paradigms. Some basic things we need to stay firm on are the following:

- Gender is binary
- Gender differences are real and God-given, and to be celebrated, not suppressed
- Sexual expression is legitimate only in the context of an Islāmically valid relationship between a man and a woman
- We need to actively critique and deconstruct the Western paradigm of sexuality and show its flaws

In modern times, Western colonization has shifted its focus from military domination to ideological control. One example of this is the exportation of Western sexual ideologies to many Muslim countries, despite the fact that their own sexual paradigm is plagued with chaos. Unfortunately, the defeatist mentality of some Muslim countries has allowed those ideologies to take root in their societies, leading to a devastating effect on Muslim marriages, among other things.

[175] Also statistically, few people try and have a great marital life, please refer to the Podcast: A Way Beyond the Rainbow Podcast, Dr. Waheed Jensen (88 episodes, 2020–2022) where he discussed these things in detail.

Rejection at the community level of the sexual identity paradigm

We must once again separate desires, actions, and identities.

Terminological implications → avoid identity-laden vocabulary: gay, LGBTQI+, dignifying "who people **are**," etc.

Use descriptive terms instead, and *adjectives* not nouns: "has homosexual feelings," "experiences same-sex attraction/gender dysphoria."

No gay exceptionalism (either positive or negative)

Pushing acceptance of LGBTQI+ acts in an Islāmic environment is just as unacceptable as pushing alcohol, zinā, etc.

Maintaining the Straight Path: Clarity, Compassion, Conviction

You are not more merciful than Allāh. True compassion is guiding one to the truth and what pleases the Creator. Be humble and kind, but never apologetic or embarrassed about our Islāmic beliefs. Islāmic teachings on gender and sexual ethics are not an embarrassment or a problem; they are the only solution!

5. **Should Muslims consider biological sex as the gender of a person before and/or after gender reassignment surgery?**

On what other grounds would a Muslim consider a person's gender to be based off of? Sex-change surgery does not actually change one's sex; it is a cosmetic alteration. For women, it usually involves breast reduction and contouring to appear more masculine, and for men, it involves castrating and refashioning the removed male genitalia to look more feminine.

For the legal ruling (ḥukum) on gender reassignment surgeries, the Fiqh Council of North America, in accordance with all mainstream fiqh scholarly bodies around the world, has deemed that it is impermissible to actively attempt to change one's biological sex/gender. This is whether it is done through hormone treatment, surgical procedures, or any combination of the two. All mechanisms for seeking to actively transition from one sex/gender to another are forbidden according to the teachings of Islām.

The only exception to this—if it even is deemed an exception—is when an intersex person undergoes surgery to bring his or her physiology more in line with the gender which he or she has been determined to belong to more closely.[176]

6. **If a trans person comes to the masjid, where should they pray?**

Trans individuals should have a private area to pray in, ideally somewhere not in the main rows, somewhere in between the men and the women, but in a separate row because of ambiguity, as suggested by classical fiqh scholars like Ibn-Qudāmah.[177]

7. **Should trans people be allowed to use restrooms in the masjid according to their self-identified gender?**

I do not see how this free-intermixing can be accommodated in Islamic Centers. So-called trans women, (biological males who imitate women) often have an underlying erotic fetish. These are men who are aroused by becoming women, and this psychological condition, known as autogynephilia, is not uncommon. A simple google search can manifest that.

---

[176] https://muslimmatters.org/2022/06/21/fatwa-regarding-transgenderism/
[177] Dr. Hatem El-Haj, Sharh Umdah al Fiqh, 1\136

Putting these men in the same restrooms as our mothers and daughters is, and should be, completely out of bounds.

The easiest and best solution is to allow such individuals to use single stall bathrooms. Although not every masjid will have a single stall bathroom, the chances are that a trans person will attempt to attend a larger masjid in suburban areas, and those masjids usually have at least one bathroom that is single stall. Providing them access to that single stall bathroom seems to be the most prudent solution and Allah knows the best

8. Is a nikāḥ valid between a trans person and someone of the same biological sex? Does it matter if their marriage was done before they converted?

A nikāḥ between a trans person and someone of the same biological sex is completely and unambiguously impermissible and invalid. It is essentially a gay/lesbian marriage, and is unquestionably ḥarām and invalid in the strongest possible terms. Permitting this would be doing istiḥlāl (the act of regarding something as permissible, or ḥalāl, although it is ḥarām) of something that is impermissible, and whose impermissibility is from the ma'lūm min al-dīn bi-ḍarūra (Necessarily known to be part of the religion).

Marriage is a legal contract between a man and woman under Islāmic law, by means of which she becomes permissible for him and vice versa. As for a marriage between a man and another man, or between a woman and another woman, that is not considered to be marriage based on the above definition. Rather, it is one of the worst and most abhorrent of immoral and shameful deeds in Islāmic law. It is not permissible for a Muslim who believes in Allāh and the Last Day to engage in it.

إِنَّهُ كَانَ فَاحِشَةً وَمَقْتًا وَسَاءَ سَبِيلًا

"Indeed, it was an immorality and hateful [to Allāh] and was evil as a way"[178]

If their marriage was done before they converted, it should be treated just like a gay marriage before a gay person converted (i.e., invalid).[179]

9. How will the inheritance of a trans-person be distributed?

According to their biological sex. Also, can you just imagine how many people can potentially abuse this if we consider their gender after the surgery that they will play around the Islāmic law and get more wealth?

10. What is the ruling on marrying a man who is intersex? Is there a difference between an intersex person and modern-day trans person from an Islāmic perspective?

The first thing to note, and perhaps the most important disclaimer, is that intersex (or a true hermaphrodite) is considered to be different from transgender. With advances in medicine, the determination of sex is much easier. The incidence of intersex persons with completely ambiguous genitalia is extremely rare. This condition used to be referred to as being a "true hermaphrodite" in the medical literature.[180]

---

[178] Surah An-Nisā`, Verse 22

[179] Dealing with the converts: We might not confront such a person on Day 1 after converting, though at some point I imagine we would have to guide such a person to live in accordance with Allāh's command because Allāh's laws won't be amended based on the feelings of individuals, rather it should be the other way around.

[180] Sharh Umdah, Dr. hatem, 2\564

The word “khunthā”[181] (translated here as “intersex”) applies to a person who cannot be easily characterized as male or female, or one who has both male and female anatomy.

In Islāmic law, it refers to one who has the anatomy of both male and female, or one who has neither reproductive organs, but has an orifice through which they urinate.

The word “mukhannath”[182] (“effeminate”) refers to a person who behaves like a woman in gentleness, speech, appearance, movements, and so on.

Effeminate people are of two types:

(i) Those who are having effeminate traits; there is no sin on them.

(ii) Those who were not having effeminate traits; rather they choose to imitate women in their movements and speech. This is not permissible, and the Prophet (صلى الله عليه وسلم) cursed men who imitate women and women who imitate men.[183]

The mukhannath, or effeminate man, is one who is obviously male, unlike the khunthā (intersex), which are ambiguous.

Intersex people may be divided into two categories, ambiguous (مشكل) and unambiguous (غير مشكل).

(a) The unambiguous intersex individual is one who shows clear indications of being either male or female, so it is known that this person is a man or a woman (from appearances). There is

181 خنثى
182 مخنث

183 Al-Bukhari

no ambiguity involved here; rather this is a man who has something extra that was created in him, or a woman who has something extra that was created in her.

(b) The ambiguous intersex individual is one who shows no clear indications of being either male or female (in appearance), and does not know whether they are a man or a woman, or has characteristics of both genders. This requires more detail.

This ambiguity is of two further types:

a) one that has the anatomy of both genders, where other defining characteristics are present in equal measure.

b) one who does not have the anatomy of either; rather they have an orifice through which they urinate.

The majority of scholars are of the view that intersex individuals that, before puberty, urinate from a penis, are considered by Islāmic law to be boys. And intersex individuals, before puberty, that urinate like girls, they are considered by Islāmic law to be girls.

After puberty, the matter is to be decided by one of the following signs:

If the individual begins to grow a beard, ejaculates, impregnates a woman, or has intercourse with a woman, he is legally considered a man. This is proof of his masculinity, as was mentioned by a number of scholars.[184]

---

[184] Al-Haskafi, Ad-Durar Al-Mukhtar Sharh Tanveer Al-Absaar wa Jaami' Al-Behar & Molana Ashraf Ali Thanwi, Imdad-ul-Fatwa, 2\286 & As-Sarkhasi, Al-Mabsoot, 7\285

If this individual grows breasts that produce milk, or menstruates, or it is possible to have intercourse with them, then this person is legally considered a woman. If this individual give birth, then she is definitely considered a female, and this factor is to be given precedence over all other indications to the contrary.[185]

Also, if such a person says that they are sexually attracted to both or neither genders, then the matter remains ambiguous[186],[187].

Now to answer this question regarding the marriage of one who is genuinely intersex. If it is an unambiguous case, then according to how he or she is classified, he or she may marry someone of the opposite gender. If it is an ambiguous case, then the marriage of such a person cannot be valid (just like there is an ambiguity in the case of a transgender individual). The reason being that he or she may be either gender, in which case how can they marry another male or female, which could result in a "marriage" between individuals of the same gender.

Ibn Qudāmah Al-Ḥanbali said:

"One who is intersex must be either ambiguous or unambiguous. If he is not ambiguous, in the sense that he has male characteristics, then he is a man and comes under the rulings on men; if this person has female characteristics, then she is a woman and comes under the rulings on women. If he is ambiguous, with no signs of being either male or female, in this case, marriage is not valid for him, and he should not marry either a woman or a man. But in that case, what should he do if he has sexual desire? The answer is that we should

185 As-Suyuti, Al-Ashbah Wa-Nazaair, Page 242

186 The term bisexual was not evolved back in the days. Also again I want to remind all the readers that this is for intersex who are naturally born that way and not transgender.

187 al-Mawsoo'ah al-Fiqhiyyah, 20/21-23

tell him: Be patient until Allāh changes your condition to something better. (we can also add that this world is a place of tests, and tests related to our sexual desires is quite difficult. Each test will be a different test for different people regarding sexual desires, so never seek to justify your desires and disobey Allāh by fulfilling your desires in a way which is not compatible with the Islāmic paradigm of sexuality).[188]

One of the famous Ḥanbali scholars, Shaykh Muḥammad ibn Ṣāliḥ al-'Uthaymeen said:

"With regard to the marriage of an ambiguously intersex individual who has both male and female anatomy – that is, he has a penis like a male and vulva like a female, and it is not clear whether he is male or female, such as if he can urinate both like a man and like a woman, and there is no other sign to determine whether he is male or female – in this case, marriage is not valid for him, and he should not marry either a woman or a man. He should not marry a female because of the possibility that he may be female, and a female cannot marry another female; nor should he marry a male because of the possibility that he may be male, and a male cannot marry another male. In this case, he should remain unmarried until the matter becomes clear; when it becomes clear, if he is male then he may marry a female, and if he is female then she may marry a male. The ruling is that marriage is temporarily forbidden, until the matter becomes clear."[189]

To summarize: in the case of an intersex individual, if it is not known whether they are male or female, it is not permissible for them to get married; if it becomes clear that he is male or female, then marriage becomes valid, so long as they seek advice in such a matter

[188] Ibn Qudamah, Al-Mughni, 7\619
[189] ash-Sharh al-Mumti', 12/160

from a Sharī'ah-complaint Muslim therapist, or trustworthy Muslim doctor who specializes in such matters, in order to confirm their biological (sex) and the possibility of marriage.[190]

Also, the term "trans" as it is used in today's culture does not equate to the discussion in the books of Islāmic law on khunthā. Specifically, as we have seen, the phenomenon of intersex, which is what legal discussions of the khunthā in Islāmic law are about, stems from a physiological abnormality that renders the individual's classification as male or female objectively ambiguous. By contrast, current-day transgenderism references a psychological condition in which the trans individual subjectively does not identify with the gender of the unambiguously male or female body with which he or she was born. And Allāh knows best.

11. Should Muslim scholars and leaders outsource people struggling with gender dysphoria to psychologists who often support their transition?

Absolutely not, because we know that most therapists are leftists and Freudists in their worldview. Muslims need to invest in alternative spaces with counselors, psychologists, and therapists who are independently funded by the community, who know therapy professionally with an Islāmic worldview, and who can operate without worrying about their license as a counselor or therapist being revoked. As advising against transitioning may carry such consequences in a professional capacity.

[190] For more details, Pls read: مجلة المجمع الفقهي الإسلامي، ص 355

12. Should Muslims object to pronoun identification introductions in Muslim spaces like MSAs, etc.?

For Muslim spaces, this must be the case. Muslims should not follow these LGBTQI+ activist fads, which only normalize their worldview and promote their movement.

Similarly, we should not use other vocabulary and language fads that commit us to problematic metaphysical assumptions of the LGBTQI+ movement, such as affirming that trans women are women (or trans men are men), conceding a normative distinction between sex and gender, using de-gendered terminology for inherently and normatively gendered realities (like saying "pregnant people" to avoid saying "pregnant women," on the grounds that "not all people who are pregnant are women"), and other such Orwellian nonsense. In fact, we should try our best to avoid the use of the LGBTQI+ acronym altogether, speaking instead in more clinical (rather than identarian) terms for things like "homosexuality" or "same-sex attraction," gender identity issues, etc.

Bibliography and works cited:
English work:

1) Carl Trueman, Strange New World, Crossway, Wheaton, IL, 2022

2) Stephen Hicks, Explaining Postmodernism, Scholarly Publishing, Tempe, Arizona, New Berlin / Milwaukee, 2004

3) Dr. Israr Ahmed, Islamic Renaissance - The real task Ahead, Lahore MARKAZI ANJUMAN KDAM-UL-QUR'AN 2001

4) Robert N.Bellah et al., Habits of the Heart: Individualism and commitment in American life (Berkeley: University of California Press, 1996)

5) Millman, History of Christianity, Paris, A and W Galignani And co., No. 18, Rue Viveenne, 1840

6) Will Durant, The Reformation. New York, Simon and Schuster, 1980

7) W. T. Jones, A History of Western Philosophy, vol. 2, The Medieval Mind (New York: Harcourt, Brace, Jovanovich, 1969),

8) Malcolm Lambert, Medieval Heresy: Popular Movements from the Gregorian Reform to the Reformation (Malden, MA.: Blackwell Publishing, 2002)

9) Andrew Coulson, *Market Education: The Untold History* (New Brunswick: Transaction Publishers, 1999), pp. 58–60. Also read: Richard Rubenstein, *Aristotle's Children: How Christians, Muslims and Jews Rediscovered Ancient Wisdom and Illuminated the Middle Ages* (New York: Harcourt, Inc., 2003),

10) Richard Rubenstein, Aristotle's Children: How Christians, Muslims and Jews Rediscovered Ancient Wisdom and Illuminated the Middle Ages (New York: Harcourt, Inc., 2003),

11) Charles Freeman, The Closing of the Western Mind: The Rise of Faith and the Fall of Reason (New York: Vintage Books, 2005)

12) Angus Maddison, Phases of Capitalist Development (New York: Oxford University Press, 1982),

13) Angus Maddison, The World Economy: A Millennial Perspective (Paris: Organization for Economic Cooperation and Development, 2001),

14) Andrew Bernstein, The Capitalist Manifesto: The Historic, Economic and Philosophic Case for Laissez-Faire (Lanham, Md.: 2005),

15) Will Durant, The Story of Civilization, vol. 4, The Age of Faith (New York: Simon & Schuster, 1950),

16) Peter Gay, The Enlightenment: An Interpretation, 2 vols. (New York: Knopf, 1966, 1969).

17) Hans Krippenberg, Changing world religion map. Sacred places, identities, Practices and Politics

18) West, Henry R. and Duignan, Brian. "utilitarianism". Encyclopedia Britannica, 19 Oct. 2022,

19) Wilhelm Reich, The Sexual Revolution: Toward a self-regulating character structure, trans. Therese Pol, (NY: Farrar, Straus, and Giroux, 1974)

20) Rene Descartes, Discourse on the method and principles of philosophy, First principle, The Project Gutenberg EBook, 2016

21) Rene Descartes, Meditations on First Philosophy, trans: John Cottingham, Cambridge university press, 2017

22) Jean-Jacques Rousseau: The Social Contract and other later political writings, ed. And trans. Victor Gourevitch, Cambridge Texts in the history of political thought (Cambridge: Cambridge university press, 1997)

23) Jean-Jacques Rousseau, Confessions, ed. Patrick Coleman, Trans. Angela Scholar (Oxford: Oxford University press, 2000)

24) Jean-Jacques Rousseau: The Discourses and Other Early Political Writings, ed. And trans. Victor Gourevitch, Cambridge Texts in the history of Political thought (Cambridge: Cambridge University Press, 1997)

25) Yuval Levin, A time to build, From Family and community to congress and the campus, How recommitting to our institutions can revive the American dream, (NY: Basic books, 2020)

26) Karl Marx and Friedrich Engels, Marx on Religion, ed. John Raines (Philadelphia, PA: Temple University Press, 2002)

27) Friedrich Nietzsche, The Gay science, trans. Walter Kaufmann (NY: Vintage, 1974)

28) Sigmund Freud, Civilizations and its discontents, trans. James Strachey (NY: W.W. Norton, 1989)

29) Sigmund Freud, Three Essays on the Theory of sexuality, trans. and ed. James Strachey (NY: Basic books, 2000)

30) Saint Augustine, The Confessions, Hackett Publishing Company, Inc., 2006

31) Simone De Beauvior, The Second Sex, trans. Constance Borde and Sheila Malovany-Chevallier, with an introduction by Judith Thurman (NY: Vintage, 2011)

32) Janice Raymond, Transsexual empire - The making of the she-male, (NY: Teachers college Press 1994)

33) Dr. Hatem Al-Haj, Love and Hate, Independently published, February 26, 2022

34) Merrick, C. (2019). Hating Evil: Understanding the Role of Evil in Interpersonal Hate. *Graduate Theses and Dissertations* Retrieved from https://scholarworks.uark.edu/etd/3380

35) Jean Piaget, The Moral Judgment of the Child, trans. Marjorie Gabain, 5th impr. (London: Routledge & Kegan Paul, 1968)

36) Greene, J. and Haidt, J. (2002) How (and Where) Does Moral Judgment Work? Trends in Cognitive Sciences, 6, 517-523. http://dx.doi.org/10.1016/S1364-6613(02)02011-9

37) Barbara Herman, "The Practice of Moral Judgment, The Harvard University press, 1996

38) Carl Sherif El-Tobgui, Reason, "Revelation & the Reconstitution of Rationality: Taqī al-Dīn Ibn Taymiyya''s (d. 728/1328) Dar' Ta'ārud al-'Aql wa-l-Naql or 'The refutation of the contradiction of reason and revelation'" (PhD Thesis, McGill University, 2013)

39) Gordon Pennycook, Jonathan A. Fugelsang, and Derek J. Koehler, "Everyday Consequences of Analytic Thinking," Current Directions in Psychological Science 24, no. 6 (2015), http://www.jstor.org/stable/44318881

40) Foucault, Michel. The History of Sexuality, Volume 1, an introduction. Translated by Robert Hurley. Random House, 1978

41) Foucault, Michel. Madness and Civilization. Translated by Richard Howard. Random, 1965

42) Dworkin Andrea, Intercourse, Newyork: Free Press 1987

43) Fish Stanley, Is there a text in this Class? Harvard University Press, 1982

44) Fish Stanley, Pragmatism and Literary Theory, Critical Inquiry 11. March 1985,

45) Lentricchia Frank, Criticism and Social change, University of Chicago 1983

46) Mackinnon Catharine, Only Words. Harvard University 1993

47) Stephen White, Political Theory and Postmodernism. Cambridge University Press, 1991

48) Stewart E. Kelly, Understanding Postmodernism: A Christian perspective, IVP Academic 2017

Arabic Books:

1. ابن تيمية، مجموع الفتاوى، مجمع الملك فهد، المدينة المنورة، المملكة العربية السعودية، 1995 م.
2. القاطرجي، الشذوذ الجنسي في الفكر الغربي وأثره على العالم العربي، مركز الفكر الغربي
3. الدوسري، تقديم لوط ابنتيه لقومه في التوراة والقرآن، تكوين السعودية، 2022
4. الآجري، ذم اللواط، دار اللولؤة، 2022
5. ابن تيمية، قتال الكفار ومهادنتهم، 2004
6. القرافي، الذخيرة، بيروت، 1994
7. ابن دقيق العيد، إحكام الأحكام، مطبع السنة المحمدية، القاهرة
8. ابن بطال، شرح صحيح البخاري، مكتبة الرشد، الرياض، 2003
9. ابن قيم، روضة المحبين ونزهة المشتاقين، دار الكتب العلمية، بيروت، 1983 م.
10. ابن حزم، طوق الحمامة في الألفة والألاف، المؤسسة العربية، بيروت، 1987 م.
11. ابن القطان، إحكام النظر في أحكام النظر، دار القلم، دمشق، 2012 م
12. ابن قيم، أحكام أهل الذمة، 1997
13. ابن عاشور، التحرير والتنوير، بيروت
14. الطحاوي، عقيدة الطحاوية، بيروت، 1414هـ
15. العزالي، إحياء علوم الدين، دار المعارفة، بيروت،
16. الطيار، الموسوعة التفسير بالماثور، السعودية، 2019

17. الطريفي، العقلية الليبرالية في رصف العقل ووصف النقل، دار المنهاج، السعودية، 1434 هـ

18. سعيد بن علي القحطاني، الاختلاط بين الرجال والنساء، مؤسسة الجريسي للتوزيع والإعلان، 1432 هـ

19. خالد بن عثمان، الاختلاط بين الجنسين في الميزان، مكتبة دار المنهاج، الرياض، 1433 هـ.

20. أبي نصر محمد بن عبد الله، الاختلاط أصل الشر في دمار الأمم الأسر، دار الآثار، صنعاء، 2009 م.

21. محمد صابر عبد الدايم إبراهيم، الليبرالية وأثرها على الدعوة الإسلامية، رسالة دكتوراة، المكتبة الأزهرية للتراث، 2016 م

22. الندوي، ماذا خسر العالم بانحطاط المسلمين، دار القلم – دمشق، 2021 م

23. الحصكفي، الدرر المختار شرح تنوير الأبصار وجامع البحار، 2006 هـ

24.

25. علي بن عبد الله، إشكال وجوابه في حديث أم حرام بنت ملحان، دار المحدث، 1425 هـ،

26. محمد بن إسماعيل البخاري، صحيح البخاري، دار طوق النجاة، 1422 هـ.

27. ابن حجر، فتح الباري، دار المعرفة، بيروت، 1379 م.

28. ابن منظور، لسان العرب، دار صادر، بيروت، 1414 هـ

29. ابراهيم مصطفى، المعجم الوسيط، دار الدعوة

30. محمد بن إسماعيل، عودة الحجاب، دار طيبة، 2007 م.

31. بكر أبو زيد، حراسة الفضيلة، دار العاصمة، رياض، 2005 م.
32. عبد العزيز البداح، تحريم الاختلاط والرد على من أباحه، 2011 م.
33. النووي، المجموع شرح المهذب، المكتبة العصرية، بيروت، 2014 م.
34. عبد العزيز كامل، معركة الثوابت بين الإسلام والليبرالية، البيان الرياض
35. ابن قيم، إعلام الموقعين عن رب العالمين، دار الكتب العلمية، 1991 م.
36. وزارة الأوقاف والشئون الإسلامية، الموسوعة الفقهية الكويتية، دار السلاسل، الكويت، 1427
37. ابن نجيم، غمز عيون البصائر شرح الكتاب الأشباه والنظائر، دار الكتب العلمية، دار الباز، 1985
38. صالح عبد السميع، جواهر الإكليل شرح مختصر الشيخ خليل، المكتبة الثقافية، بيروت
39. النووي، روضة الطالبين وعمدة المفتين، المكتب الإسلامي، 1991
40. ابن إدريس البهوتي، كشاف القناع عن متن الإقناع، عالم الكتب، بيروت، 1983
41. ابن الهمام الحنفي، شرح فتح القدير مع تكملة نتائج الأفكار، المطبعة الكبرى الأميرية، 1315 هـ
42. عثمان بن علي الحنفي، تبيين الحقائق شرح كنز الدقائق، المطبعة الكبرى الأميرية، 1313 هـ
43. أبو العباس المالكي، الشرح الصغير، دار المعارف
44. الشربيني، مغني المحتاج إلى معرفة معاني ألفاظ المنهاج، دار الكتب العلمية، بيروت، 2000

45. القرطبي، الجامع الأحكام القرآن، دار الكتب المصرية، 1964
46. الرازي، مفاتيح الغيب (تفسير الرازي)، دار إحياء التراث العربي، بيروت، 1420 هـ
47. النيسابوري، صحيح مسلم، دار إحياء التراث العربي، بيروت
48. أبو داود، سنن أبو داود، المكتبة العصرية، صيدا، بيروت
49. السرخسي شمس الدين، المبسوط، دار المعرفة، بيروت، 1989
50. أحمد الدرير الدسوقي، حاشية الدسوقي على الشرح الكبير، عيسى البالي الحلبي، 2015
51. ابن حمزة الشهاب الدين الرملي، نهاية المحتاج إلى شرح المنهاج، درا الفكر، بيروت، 1984
52. ابن النجيم المصري، البحر الرائق شرح كنز الدقائق، دار الكتاب الإسلامي، دار الكتاب الإسلامي
53. أبو الحسن البصري الماوردي، الحاوي الكبير، دار الكتب العلمية، بيروت، لبنان، 1999 م
54. علاء الدين المرداوي الحنبلي، الإنصاف في معرفة الراجح من الخلاف، دار إحياء التراث العربي.
55. مصطفي بن سعد السيوطي الدمشقي الحنبلي، مطالب أولى النهى في شرح غاية المنتهى، المكتب الإسلامي، 1994 م
56. ابن قدامة، المغني، مكتبة القاهرة، 1968 م.

57. ابن حجر الهيتمي الشافعي، تحفو المحتاج في شرح المنهاج، المكتبة التجارية الكبرى بمصر، 1983 م.
58. عبد الغني بن طالب الدمشقي الحنفي، اللباب في شرح الكتاب، المكتبة العلمية، بيروت، لبنان
59. النووي، المنهاج شرح صحيح مسلم، دار إحياء التراث العربي، بيروت، 1392 ه
60. السيوطي، الأشباه النظائر، دار الكتب العلمين، 1990 م.
61. شمس الدين الرملي الشافعي، نهاية المحتاج إلى شرح المنهاج، دار الفكر، بيروت، 1984 م.
62. محمد بن صالح العثيمين، مجموع أسئلة تهم الأسرة المسلمة، دار الوطن
63. أبو عبد الله الخرشي المالكي، شرح مختصر خليل، دار الفكر، بيروت
64. أبو بكر الدمياطي، إعانة الطالبين على حل ألفاظ فتح المبين، دار الفكر، 1997 م.
65. الراغب الأصفهاني، المفردات في غريب القرآن، دار القلم، دمشق، 1412 ه.
66. محمد الزرقاني المصري الأزهري، شرح الزرقاني على موطأ الإمام مالك، مكتبة الثقافية الدينية، القاهرة، 2003 م.
67. النووي، الأذكار، دار الفكر، بيروت، 1994 م.
68. أبو الفضل العراقي، طرح التثريب في شرح التقريب، دار إحياء التراث العربي
69. الطبراني، معجم الكبير، مكتبة ابن تيمية، القاهرة، 1994 م.
70. الكاساني، بدائع الصنائع في ترتيب الشرائع، دار الكتب العلمية، 1986 م.

71. أحمد بن غانم النفراوي المالكي، الفواكه الدواني على رسالة ابن أبي زيد القيرواني، دار الفكر، 1995 م.
72. الشمس الدين الرملي، نهاية محتاج إلى شرح المنهاج، دار الفكر، 1984
73. أبو بكر الحسيني الحصني الشافعي، كفاية الأخيار في حل غاية الإختصار، دار الخير، دمشق، 1994 م.
74. ابن عابدين، الدر المختار وحاشية ابن عابدين، دار الفكر، بيروت، 1992 م.
75. أبو عيسى الترمذي، سنن الترمذي، دار الغرب الإسلامي، بيروت، 1998 م.
76. ابن ماجه، سنن ابن ماجه، دار إحياء الكتب العربية، الحلبي.
77. بدر الدين العيني، عمدة القاري شرح صحيح البخاري، دار إحياء التراث العربي، بيروت.
78. البيهقي، معرفة السنن والآثار، جامع الدراسات الإسلامية، كراتشي، باكستان، 1991 م.
79. ابن كثير، البداية والنهاية، دار إحياء التراث العربي، 1988 م.
80. أبو الفلاح الحنبلي، شذرات الذهب في أخبار من ذهب، دار ابن كثير، دمشق، 1986 م.
81. الذهبي، سير الأعلام النبلاء، دار الحديث، القاهرة، 2006 م.
82. النسائي، سنن النسائي، مكتب المطبوعات الإسلامية، حلب، 1986 م.
83. ابن أبي جمرة، بهجة النفوس وتحليها بمعرفة مالها وما عليها، مطبعة الصدق الخيرية، الأزهر، 1348 هـ.

84. ابن بطال، شرح صحيح البخاري لابن بطال، مكتبة الرشد، السعودية، الرياض، 2003 م.
85. مالك، موطأ، مؤسسة زايد بن سلطان آل نهيان للأعمال الخيرية والإنسانية، أبو طبي، الإمارات، 2004 م.
86. المباركفوري، تحفة الأحوذي بشرح جامع الترمذي، دار الكتب العلمية، بيروت.
87. أحمد، مسند أحمد، مؤسسة الرسالة، 2001 م.
88. ابن عبد البر القرطبي، التمهيد لما في الموطأ مع المعاني والأسانيد، وزارة عموم الأوقاف والشؤون الإسلامية، المغرب، 1387 هـ.
89. الشنقيطي، أضواء البيان في إيضاح القرآن بالقرآن، دار الفكر، بيروت، 199 5 م.
90. علي بن أبي بكر برهان الدين، الهداية في شرح بداية المبتدي، دار إحياء التراث العربي، بيروت، 2010 م.